HOLY WARRIORS, INFIDELS, AND PEACEMAKERS IN AFRICA

Holy Warriors, Infidels, and Peacemakers in Africa

Yacob Tesfai

palgrave
macmillan

First published in 2010 by
PALGRAVE MACMILLAN®
in the United States—a division of St. Martin's Press LLC,
175 Fifth Avenue, New York, NY 10010.

Where this book is distributed in the UK, Europe and the rest of the world,
this is by Palgrave Macmillan, a division of Macmillan Publishers Limited,
registered in England, company number 785998, of Houndmills,
Basingstoke, Hampshire RG21 6XS.

Palgrave Macmillan is the global academic imprint of the above companies
and has companies and representatives throughout the world.

Palgrave® and Macmillan® are registered trademarks in the United States,
the United Kingdom, Europe and other countries.

ISBN: 978–0–230–10427–3

Library of Congress Cataloging-in-Publication Data

Tesfai, Yacob.
    Holy warriors, infidels, and peacemakers in Africa / Yacob Tesfai.
        p. cm.
    ISBN 978–0–230–10427–3 (hardback)
        1. Africa—Religion. 2. Violence—Africa. 3. Religion and
politics—Africa. 4. Violence—Religious aspects. I. Title.

BL2400.T46 2010
306.6096'09045—dc22   2009050856

A catalogue record of the book is available from the British Library.

Design by Newgen Imaging Systems (P) Ltd., Chennai, India.

First edition: June 2010

10 9 8 7 6 5 4 3 2 1

Printed in the United States of America.

CONTENTS

QUESTIONS TO PONDER

"Exuding haughty self-contentment, [Charles] Taylor (former President of Liberia) seated himself in a high-backed rattan chair...When he began to speak it was, as usual, pure bombast.

'We must take a moment to thank God,' he said, *'for this popular, people's uprising was, in reality, God's war...'* Almost every Liberian had lost his livelihood...People were living in abject poverty and degradation, without a formal economy or even a government. For all of this, the only thing Taylor saw fit to say about the destruction he had wrought was that it had been God's plan."

"*'Isn't it outrageous for someone who has drugged small boys, given them guns and trained them to kill to call this God's war?'* I asked... *'How dare you call the destruction of your country in this manner and the killing of two hundred thousand people God's war?'*"

"In truth it wasn't really a question, but Taylor knew that he couldn't allow this to be the last word. *'I just believe in the destiny of man being controlled by God, and wars, whether man-made or what, are directed by a force,'* he sputtered, momentarily confused. *'And so when I say it is God's war, God has his own way of restoring the land, and he will restore it after this war.'*" (French 2005: 109–110)

PREFACE

THE BULK OF THE MATERIAL FOR THIS BOOK BEGAN TO BE BROUGHT together during three research study trips that I undertook at the Institute for Social Studies (ISS) at The Hague, The Netherlands. The stays, which added up to approximately six months, were undertaken in three separate times: May–July 2004, November 2004–January 2005, and February–March 2006.

The research carried out in these study trips was the continuation and culmination of a long engagement with the issues of religion, society, and violent conflicts. These topics have been close to me personally, professionally, and intellectually over a period of more than thirty years. To begin with, on the personal level, the Horn of Africa region has been a theater of violent conflicts for many years. Consequently, being born and having lived in this area raises questions about the meaning of violent conflicts.

On the professional level, I struggled with the effects of war from 1977 to 1987 when it was raging in the region (Dawit 1989; Wrong 2005: 237). By virtue of my position as the General Secretary of the Evangelical Church of Eritrea (ECE) and general overseer and responsible for the activities of the Lutheran World Federation/Department of World Service (LWF/DWS)—Ethiopia Office in Eritrea, the question of the role of Faith-based Organizations (FBOs) in the context of war assumed crucial importance. What should FBOs do in such a situation? How do they interpret war in the light of their faith? How do they react to the devastating consequences of war: increased poverty, displacement, health problems, trauma, and so on? How do they relate to the warring sides? What role was religion playing in the wars? These were pertinent questions that were raised by the prevailing situation.

After ten years of engagement in this situation, I was appointed research professor at the Institute for Ecumenical Research in Strasbourg,

France. This new position offered me an opportunity to reflect on the topics in a calm and ideal environment. Besides the research work and lectures, I traveled extensively and interacted with many scholars and people from all walks of life.

This intellectual side of my research was further augmented and deepened following my appointment in October 2004 as the Senior Research Officer at the Life and Peace Institute/Horn of Africa Programme (LPI/HAP) based in Nairobi. The Institute was established in part to study and address the questions of religion and violent conflicts and their resolution. One of the topics on which it focused was "the role of religion in conflict and peace." The first meeting on this very topic in which I participated took place in Soedersoepingsbrun, Sweden. It was organized by the LPI. Another source was the Inter-Faith Action for Peace in Africa (IFAPA) that will be dealt with in the last chapter. I attended the second meeting, which was held in South Africa in April 2005. Yet another opportunity was made available to me in connection with the Global Partnership for the Prevention of Armed Conflict (GPPAC). The former United Nations (UN) Secretary-General, Mr. Kofi Anan, had strenuously advocated the need for a transition from "a culture of violence" to a "culture of peace." In this connection, he made a call to concerned civil society groups all over the world to link up with governments and the UN to address effectively the issues of violent conflicts and peace.[1] This call was picked up by the European Centre for Conflict Prevention (ECCP) based in Utrecht, The Netherlands, which assumed the task of coordination. A global conference was held at the UN Headquarters in New York, USA, in July 2006.

FBOs played a role in this conference. As part of it, LPI and the World Conference of Religions for Peace (WCRP) had assumed the task of organizing a workshop involving religious leaders. All in all, approximately twenty-five representatives from a variety of religious groups from different parts of the world took part in the workshop: Baha'is, Buddhists, Christians (a variety of denominations), Hindus, Jews, and Muslims. The group struggled with the issues of religion and violent conflicts and the contributions of FBOs to peace. I was privileged to cochair the three-day workshop.

During my time with LPI/HAP, I had the privilege of working with Christians and Muslims who were interested in these issues. Memorable among them were the meetings we held in Juba (the main—capital—city of South Sudan) and Kadugli, the Nuba Mountains, Sudan.

In Juba, a meeting was organized that brought together Muslim and Christian leaders in the city. After the sudden death of the Sudan Peoples Liberation Movement/Army (SPLM/A) leader, Dr. John Garang, in a helicopter crash, violence erupted in Juba. Another meeting was held in Jinja, Uganda. LPI/HAP brought together Christians and Muslims from south Sudan for an in-depth discussion on some aspects of the very issues dealt with in this book. The proceedings of the meeting were later published in a book that I edited (Tesfai 2006).

This book is intended to reach a wide readership that I have called here and elsewhere "middle rank leaders." These consist primarily of religious leaders, health workers, civil servants, religious faithful, politicians, business people, members and leaders of NGOs, both national and international. I would also include teachers, university and high school students as individuals and groups who are important players in the market of ideas. Equipping such a group of people with the necessary knowledge on these crucial topics will go a long way in generating the debate in the public square to which this work wishes to contribute. With such a target in mind, the book does not go into fine details. Rather, it tries to paint the picture in broad strokes.

The book is written in the spirit conveyed by Gregor Dallas: "Peace is fragile. Undoubtedly, the noblest activity of man [sic] is the construction of peace; after all the barbarisms, a few brave people somehow manage to make us civilized again" (2005: xiv). If it succeeds in reaching the above-mentioned group of people by providing them with the necessary information, elicits fruitful discussion/debate, and goads them as it were to undertake individual and/or collective engagement in the "civilizing project" for "the construction of peace," the writer's wishes would have been more than fulfilled.

Yacob Tesfai
November 2009
Nairobi, Kenya

ACKNOWLEDGMENTS

I WOULD LIKE TO THANK SOME OF THE PEOPLE WHO HAVE BEEN HELPFUL in the course of the writing of this book. Let me begin by thanking the friends who made my various trips to The Hague possible. This opportunity was given to me by the Dutch Interchurch Organization for Development Co-operation (ICCO). My late friend Arian Bons had arranged that I visit The Institute of Social Studies (ISS) at The Hague. Special thanks are due to Ms. Annet Ijff, Head of the Department for Africa and the Middle East at ICCO, for her strong support throughout the research work as well as her friendship, care, and kindness.

I thank Annet Ijff, Jacques and Rini Willemse, and Father Ben Engelbertink for their Dutch hospitality. I thank Professors Mohammed Salih, Karin Arts, and Rachel Kumar of the ISS for making their expertise available to me and helping me in everyway possible during my stay at The Hague. In this connection, I shall not forget the assistance that was accorded me by the library staff and secretariat of the institute.

I thank Johan Svensson, former Regional Resident Representative of LPI/HAP, for permitting me twice to continue the research at the ISS in my early days of employment with the LPI/HAP. In the final stages of the writing of the earlier draft of the manuscript, Peter Brune, the former executive director of LPI, arranged a seminar, where I was invited to present my findings before the LPI staff at the headquarters in Uppsala, Sweden. I am thankful to both Peter and Dr. Anne Kubai, the then director of research at LPI, for the opportunity. I am also thankful to Tore Samuelsson, LPI Communications officer, for all the understanding and help that he offered me in the course of the writing of the book. I thank Lt. General Lazarus Sumbeiywo, the special IGAD mediator of the Sudan Peace Process and currently the executive director of the Moi Africa Institute, Nairobi, for his friendship and invaluable support.

I would also like to mention some of my close collaborators who gave me some help in the course of the research: Prof. Margaret Gecaga and Prof.

Stephen Nyagah both of the Department of Philosophy and Religious Studies, School of Humanities and Social Sciences, Kenyatta University in Nairobi, Kenya and Mr. Abdurahman Abdullahi, Chairman of the Board of Trustees of Mogadishu University, Somalia. Special thanks are due to my former LPI colleagues Berekti Berhane, Rev. Basil Nyama, Florence Oduor, Elijah Moirongi for our journey together and Zahra Ashkir Guled for enlightenment on many things Somali.

Part of the material dealing with eastern and Horn of Africa was presented in a lecture delivered at a conference held at Tangaza College (Catholic University of Eastern Africa) in Nairobi. The various contributions were later published under the title, *Christian-Muslim Co-Existence in Eastern Africa* (Stenger 2008: 7–32). I am very grateful to the organizers for the permission to use in this book some of the material presented in the lecture.

At one point during the research process, I had the opportunity to interview two leading religious figures who, each in their own way and sometimes together, are involved in the search for peace through the organization of religious leaders in the continent. These are Sheikh Saliou Mbacké, consultant/coordinator for Inter-Faith Action for Peace in Africa (IFAPA) and Dr. Mustafa Ali, Secretary General, African Council of Religious Leaders (ACRL) and Africa Representative of the World Council Secretariat of the World Conference on Religions for Peace (WCRP). I thank them very much for giving me their time freely and allowing me to discuss with them the organizations they lead.

I thank the librarians of the AACC library, Catherine Ouma, for allowing me to make the library my second home and Esther Kahinga, for guidance in the library and for help with the computer as well as Christine Onyango for her assistance.

Thanks are due to those at Palgrave Macmillan who contributed to the publication of the work. Let me begin with the publisher/director, Steven Kennedy, who passed on the manuscript to his colleagues in New York with encouraging words. Luba Ostashevsky, the editor, played a key role in focusing my attention to the topic. It was her challenge that brought about this book. Joanna Mericle and Laura Lancaster accompanied me at some points until Chris Chappell and Sam Hasey took over at a propitious time.

Acronyms

AACC	All Africa Conference of Churches
ACRL	African Council of Religious Leaders
ANC	African National Congress
APLPI	Acholi Religious Leaders' Peace Initiative
ARS	Alliance for the Re-liberation of Somalia
ATR	African Traditional Religions
AU	African Union
CPA	Comprehensive Peace Agreement
DP	Democratic Party
ECCP	European Centre for Conflict Prevention
ECE	Evangelical Church of Eritrea
ECOWAS	Economic Community of West African States
ELF	Eritrean Liberation Front
EPLF	Eritrean People's Liberation Front
FBOs	Faith-Based Organizations
FNLA	National Front for the Liberation of Angola
FRELIMO	Liberation Front of Mozambique
GPPAC	Global Partnership for the Prevention of Armed Conflict
ICC	International Criminal Court
ICG	International Crisis Group
IFAPA	Inter-Faith Action for Peace in Africa
IGAD	Inter-Governmental Agency for Development
IPK	Islamic Party of Kenya
ISS	Institute of Social Studies
LPI	Life and Peace Institute
LPI/HAP	Life and Peace Institute/Horn of Africa Programme
LRA	Lord's Resistance Army
LWF	Lutheran World Federation
LWF/DWS	Lutheran World Federation/Department of World Service

MPLA	Popular Movement for the Liberation of Angola
NGK	Nederduitse Gereformeerde Kerk
NGO	Nongovernmental Organization
NHK	Nederduitsch Hervormde Kerk
NIF	National Islamic Front
NRM	National Resistance Movement
NSCC	New Sudan Council of Churches
NSIC	New Sudan Islamic Council
OAU	Organization of African Unity
OIC	Organization of Islamic Conference
OLF	Oromo Liberation Front
PAC	Pan-Africanist Congress
PRC	Program to Combat Racism
PROCMURA	Programme for Christian Muslim Relations in Africa
RENAMO	National Mozambican Resistance
RUF	Revolutionary United Front
SACC	South African Council of Churches
SADC	Southern African Development Community
SPLM/A	Sudan People's Liberation Movement/Army
SUPKEM	Supreme Council of Kenya Muslims
SWAPO	South West Africa People's Organization
SYC	Somali Youth Club
SYL	Somali Youth League
TFG	Transitional Federal Government
TFI	Transitional Federal Institutions
TPLF	Tigray People's Liberation Front
UDI	Unilateral Declaration of Independence
UIC	Union of Islamic Courts
UMLA	Uganda Muslim Liberation Army
UMSC	Uganda Muslim Supreme Council
UNITA	National Union for the Total Independence of Angola
UPA	Union of the People of Angola
UPC	Uganda Peoples' Congress
WCC	World Council of Churches
WCRP	World Conference on Religions for Peace
ZANU	Zimbabwe African National Union
ZANU-PF	Zimbabwe African National Union-Patriotic Front
ZAPU	Zimbabwe African People's Union

INTRODUCTION

RELIGION AND POLITICS HAVE BEEN DEFINED IN MANY DIFFERENT WAYS (Ellis and Ter Haar 2004: 13; Blakely, van Beek, and Thompson 1994; Lambeck 2002: 8–12). In what follows, religion is broadly defined as the understanding of life and the world in the light of a Higher Being or beings without which life can neither have meaning nor be explained. No human activity or happening in the world is exempted from being related to the higher Entity/entities. In such an understanding, intermediaries play a very important role. They act not only as instruments of the higher entities but also as interpreters of whatever is happening in this world in the light of the "otherworldly" and "supra-human." Such a worldview (*Weltanschauung*) encompasses all human activity.

Politics will be broadly defined as the art or science (one cannot exclude both) of creating systems through which society is organized and governed. In most cases, politics would like to portray itself as a purely human activity in contrast to religion. Politics essentially depends on the capacity of either individuals or groups of people to take the reins of power at the center of which is the exclusive control and use of the instruments of violence.

Broadly speaking, there are three dominant political ways of organizing society and monopolizing the instruments of violence. They have all to do with religion and politics. They could be summarized under theocracy, autocracy, and democracy. Theocracy claims that it is a rule that submits itself to God. All the duties and responsibilities of government are said to be carried out with reference to God. Since God is invisible, the government is run by religious leaders who claim to act on behalf of God; they claim to be his representatives. Since God is absolute, the religious leaders have also the final word on the administration of society. The "party of God" possesses the Truth (Friedman 1995).

Autocracy concentrates power in the hands of one man. It could also be a group (oligarchy) just as the notorious communist "vanguard of the revolution" that claims to rule "in the name of the people." It does not consult people on how they should be governed because it believes that it alone has the Truth (Szulc 1989). It claims to know what is good for the people. Autocracy has a theocratic nature because it believes that it is "god" with or without any need for religious explanations. It usually degenerates into dictatorship.

Finally, democracy is rule by the people on the basis of a social contract entered between the government and the governed (De Gruchy 1990: 219–232; Wiseman 1995; Oyugi, Odhiambo, Chege, and Gitongo 1988). This is usually formulated in the form of a constitution that contains the legal parameters of citizenship, its rights, obligations, and responsibilities. People rule themselves through their elected representatives who are held accountable by the people. Democracy reflects the will of the people.

In most cases, religion and politics are inseparable. Sometimes, they may try as much as possible to walk different paths. Even so, religion and politics cannot do without each other. They cross their boundaries and engage or clash with each other. Religion and politics are uneasy bedfellows, but bedfellows all the same. They cannot do without affecting each other because they deal with life and the world, which are their fields of operation. In the present discussion, religion and politics are crucial because of the fact that they have to do with the legitimate/illegitimate and exclusive use of violence.

In the contemporary world, one finds that the holy warrior occupies the center stage in religion and politics. It is the militant with a religious mission who is the dominant actor around which everything revolves. In this violence, not even the sacred places are spared. In fact they themselves have become the preferred battlefields of the holy warrior. There are many such examples. During the genocide in Rwanda, many Tutsis and moderate Hutus fled to church buildings hoping to find sanctuaries in the church. The custodians of the sacred place, in this case, the clergy, invited the *genocidaires* and delivered the "refugees of the Sacred" to orgies of massacres.

> The pattern across Rwanda was that many thousands of Tutsis sought refuge in churches or were herded there by Hutu government officials promising protection. One named Kayishema...stood accused of ordering

more than two thousand Tutsis into a Catholic Church on April 17, 1994, with a promise that he would protect them there. Instead, witnesses testified, Kayishema fired a gun in the air and ordered members of the army, the communal police, the *Interahamwe* militia and armed civilians to set upon trapped Tutsis with guns, grenades, *pangas*, machetes, spears and cudgels. (Berkeley 2001: 268)

Defilement of the sacred space has been taking place in many places. Normally, this would have been a scandal. Not any more! In the postelection skirmishes that took place in Kenya between December 2007 and January 2008, a group of terrified people who took refuge in a church building was torched to death.

It is a tragedy that shocked the entire nation and the international community. A group of armed youths protesting at the outcome of presidential elections attacked displaced families who had sought refuge in a church...and set the building on fire, killing more than 35 people. (Bill and Ngetich 2008: 18)

In the case of the Sudan, to take another example, the International Crisis Group (ICG) reported that, during the war in the south, the government "permits its security forces to bomb and attack Christian churches, schools, hospitals, and missions throughout the Nuba Mountains and the south, as well as mosques in opposition areas of eastern Sudan"(ICG 2002: 94). Opposing groups were ready to fight in the process of ownership of the sacred ground and destroy it in the process. Henceforth, the sacred has become a hostage of politics in the name of religion. The sacred space is increasingly becoming an area where violence takes place to make a political statement or to express a political opposition. The cumulative effect of such violation of the sacred is the defamation of the sacred. In all the cases that were cited, politics was religionized; there was no sanctity anymore! Religionized politics dares commit sacrilege by means of violence with impunity.

In reflecting on violence, R. Scott Appleby has written of *the ambivalence of the sacred* (2000: 10). In my opinion, he focuses more on the act of violence. He discusses the arguments for and against violence by leaders and followers of religion. Without taking great distance from Appleby's analysis, more emphasis will be put on the actor/actress instead in what follows. The ambivalence that is highlighted in this context is in connection with the actor himself/herself, the holy warrior, the one who is aspiring to attain sainthood or compliance with the will of the sacred through one's specific act of violence. The spotlight falls on the instrument of violence and the ambiguity that hangs on one's head. The ambivalence in this connection is that the holy warrior could turn out to be an infidel, one who twists and deforms the norms of the faith for which one apparently fights and for which one dies. To present the wide ranging faces of this ambivalence and the possibility of transcending it, the book is divided into the following chapters.

Chapter 1 deals with the situation that existed in South Africa before the official demise of Apartheid in 1994. The main thrust of Apartheid was constructed on the basis of religion. This religious worldview was bent on containing blacks militarily both inside and outside the country. The dominant Christian Church provided the theological rationale for the policy of Apartheid. Chapter 2 takes us to the Sudan where the mixture of religion and race has become explosive. Religion was at the center of the violence. Even though a peace agreement had been signed in 1972, the war flared up again when General Nimeiri made *Sharia* the law of the land in 1983. This project of total control of the body politic by Islamists was further strengthened with the coming to power of President Omar al-Bashir in 1989. Peace remains fragile. Chapter 3 deals with West Africa where religion-inspired violence has raged intermittently: Nigeria, Ivory Coast, Liberia, and Sierra Leone. Even after the end of the wars, religious questions still linger and cry out for attention.

Chapter 4 focuses on the eastern-Africa region: Kenya, Tanzania, and Uganda. The various interreligious relationships are explored. Chapter 5 takes us to consider the case of the Horn of Africa consisting of Djibouti, Ethiopia, Eritrea, and Somalia. Chapter 6 brings us to a special consideration of Somalia. One of the avenues to the national rehabilitation has been the introduction of a political system based on *Sharia*. The developments in Somalia have posed a new challenge to the order/disorder in the Horn. Together with the situation in the Sudan, it opened up for the region a new frontier of violent conflicts fuelled by religion. Chapter 7 looks at religious initiatives in favor of peace. It looks at the global context. Continent-wide movements such as IFAPA, ACRL, and PROCMURA are presented and discussed.

Chapter 1

Religion and Racial Differences in the South

Religion and politics were intertwined in the southern tip of Africa for many years. The white Afrikaner community had developed a worldview based on religion. All their life and political orientation was viewed in the light of the Divine. They believed that they were the recipients of a special divine dispensation that set them apart as a people. The whites believed that they had a divine right to own the land, exclude the original inhabitants, and use them as their slaves. They were fiercely attached to this religious perspective and were ready to defend it. Finally, in 1948, the policy of Apartheid was promulgated officially. This religious-political orientation had a great effect on the rest of the population of southern Africa.

On the basis of this policy, South Africa had to use violence to preserve itself and to impose its rule on others. The stronger white race saw every difference as the opposite. Separation demanded military subjugation of the other side, in this case, the blacks and the rest. There was no alternative to force since the government could not foresee the inclusion of the "inferior race."

The use of force had two targets; it was two-pronged: international and national. On the one hand, the neighboring countries were viewed as a threat to the very faith and existence of the Republic of South Africa. Being blacks themselves, they could not be seen as allies. They were believed to pose a direct challenge to its life as a special nation. Their "race," culture, way of life, and everything that made up their identity was rejected. It was contrary to what South Africans believed the measure of a human being should be. It followed that there were only two possibilities on the cards. One option was to subjugate the rest to the extent that they became weak and helpless. The other possibility was to destroy them. Violence and war were thus the only means to reach these goals. Once the excluded races began to reciprocate, violence and war became the only languages that were being used among the neighboring countries (Moorcraft 1994).

Dominated as they were by whites, South Africa, South West Africa, and Rhodesia were together in this campaign. They saw that they had to fight for their survival; theirs was a common cause. Here again, the religious card was played. They were both fighting "for the preservation of Western civilization and Christianity...To the white populations of South Africa, South West Africa, Rhodesia (later Zimbabwe) and the Portuguese colonies of Angola and Mozambique, the notion of African rule spelt disaster. All saw themselves as bastions of Western civilization, striving to uphold standards in a continent prone to strife and instability...Across Africa; a new frontier was drawn dividing the black north, from the white south, marking out southern Africa as a seemingly impregnable fortress of white power" (Meredith 2005: 116).

TOTAL WAR

Situated on the northwest of South Africa, Namibia (formerly South West Africa before 1990) was a German colony for many years. After the defeat of Germany in World War I, it was forced to withdraw from the colony that South Africa invaded and occupied during the war. The then League of Nations in 1920 and later the United Nations granted South Africa a mandate to administer it under what was termed "a trustee-ship." South Africa went ahead and incorporated the territory in 1933. The "trusteeship" was terminated in 1966 by the UN, but South Africa ignored it and introduced a lot of changes. As Basil Davidson argues, South West Africa became "in fact a South African colony where the whites ruled as permanent masters of an African population some five times their number. Here, the non-whites were to be tolerated as use-ful workers and nothing more" (Davidson 1992: 342). It followed that the white minority in the territory also adopted the system of govern-ment that obtained in South Africa. In fact, it became its province. The Apartheid system extended to Namibia (Chipenda 1991: 48–56). Even the white churches were not spared in this collaboration in segregation.

Beginning from its founding in 1966, the South West Africa People's Organization (SWAPO) posed a threat to South Africa. The latter was worried by its activities that were mainly launched from their bases in Angola where there was a proliferation of liberation movements. Some were perceived as threats to South Africa by extension since they were related to SWAPO. If and when they became independent from Portugal, they would one way or another have an influence on the larger picture. In its own way, South Africa supported the rebel groups that were sympathetic to its cause, as was the case with UNITA in Angola and RENAMO in Mozambique. Consequently, Mozambique on the northeast as well as Angola became battlefields.

ANC guerillas on their part were also operating from their bases in the neighboring countries. For this reason, ever since Mozambique and Angola attained their independence, the pressure from South Africa and Rhodesia was mounting on these countries to cut their links with the ANC and SWAPO. At the same time, RENAMO in Mozambique and UNITA in Angola were armed by South Africa to sabotage the countries' economies by the massive destruction of infrastructure such as roads, bridges, railways, and schools. The cumulative effect was that the new Mozambican government was paralyzed and weakened. It was buckling under the combined pressure of military campaigns of South Africa and the local opposition rebel group. In the end, it was forced to curtail its support for the ANC military wing. Economic and military pressure was too much to take. Samora Machel, the diehard Marxist president of the country, was left with no choice but to sign a deal with South Africa in 1984. Under similar pressure, Angola was also forced to succumb to the demands of South Africa. It signed an agreement to curb, if not to eliminate altogether, the cross-border military incursions conducted by the ANC and SWAPO guerillas.

To the west of Mozambique, Rhodesia was also burning. Rebellion had been simmering for some years. It was exacerbated in 1965 when the white minority, led by Mr. Ian Smith, defied the British colonial administration. Britain had initiated a process of finding a solution that would accommodate the black majority and the white minority. The latter were adamant in their rejection of black majority rule. Therefore, they came up with the Unilateral Declaration of Independence (UDI). Liberation movements such as Zimbabwe African National Union (ZANU) and Zimbabwe African Peoples' Union (ZAPU) took up arms to fight the white minority government.

As a result of all these military activities, war reigned supreme in the southern Africa region for a long time. Violent conflicts dominated the area up to the end of the eighties. The conflagration sucked the entire region. Even troops from Zaire were involved in supporting the South African war machine. The interesting fact is that all these wars and conflicts in all fronts were viewed as "holy" from the South African perspective. Let us first look at the local war before dealing with the religious aspect of it all.

LOCAL WAR

In this theater of war, there was the local aspect as well. The South African government was determined to put the local black population in its designated place inside or outside the country. It accomplished this feat through the system of Apartheid—separate development.[1] To start with, the nonwhite areas were divided and separated into so-called self-governing enclaves. Even though the center was not far from them, the peripheries had a semblance of "self-rule." These separate entities known as "Bantustans" or "tribal homelands" were organized on the basis of tribes. Each tribe was allocated a specific area by the central government. In theory, the tribe was responsible for running its own affairs. As a matter of fact, some of them were being coddled to opt for full "independence" as separate countries in their own right. The consequences were that such an entity had all the trappings of a "state" that was presumably responsible for governing its own people.

These fictitious states segregated on the basis of race did not have any financial or material resources of their own. They depended on handouts from the South African government. Once such "states" gained their "independence," their populations automatically lost South African citizenship; they were all disenfranchised. The end result was that South Africa would be the land of the chosen few, namely, whites only. A minority of African leaders in these Bantustans were of course benefiting from the system. Civil servants, leaders of all levels, parliamentarians, municipal workers, and others related to the "government" were treated well as long as they supported the overall strategy. However, the majority of the population suffered. They did not benefit from whatever was donated by the central authority.

As mentioned earlier, there was no lack of opposition to this political dispensation. The ANC, which was formed in 1912, was the foremost political organization that opposed the system. There were other groups such as the Communist Party and the Pan-Africanist Congress (PAC) as well, which had some commonalities and differences with the ANC in their approach to the situation. The reaction of the white authorities to these developments was swift. They unleashed massive violent repression against these movements that challenged the system.

RELIGIOUS BASIS OF THE WAR

Religion formed the basis of the system of Apartheid that obtained in South Africa. It was religion that was the main force that informed the political system. This was based on their understanding of the Christian Bible—specifically what is referred to as the Old Testament in Christian parlance—and the Jewish Scriptures.

"The traditional Afrikaner view of blacks justified by the texts taken from the Old Testament and held to be in accordance with Calvinist notions of the elect and the damned was that they were an inferior race, destined by the will of God to be hewers of wood and drawers of water. Now biblical justification was used to support the idea of a separate development. God, according to Professor Groenewald, had ordained the division of nations and wished them to be kept separate" (Meredith 1988: 47).

To begin with, the Afrikaners saw themselves as the chosen people. They were the elect people of God. In this sense, they were a special people. In expounding such a faith, they took their cue from the Israelites of old. They firmly believed that their God had chosen them and given them a special position in this particular place on earth. Special people as they are, they believed that they were called to separate themselves from all the other peoples and preserve their purity. David Lamb puts the origin of the Afrikaner ideology in graphic language:

In 1835, rifle and Bible in hand, they began moving north in small groups to escape the British and to secure a land of their own. Over the next eight years more than 12,000 *voortrekkers* (the forward trekkers, pioneers) rolled across the plains in ox wagons, headed on an uncharted course for the high veld of Natal and Transvaal provinces, firmly convinced that God had chosen to implant a new nation in Africa. On their odyssey, which became known as the Great Trek, they carried with them much bitterness and a sense of purpose forged on the anvil of oppression...In the bloodiest battle of the trek, 12,000 Zulu warriors attacked a *laager* in 1838 along the banks of the Ncome River. The 500 Boer defenders annihilated them, and keeping the vow they had made to God during the fight, built a church to commemorate the victory. The day of that victory, December 16, is celebrated today as a national holiday, the Day of the Covenant, and the Ncome in Natal province is now known as Blood River. (Lamb 1987: 324; Meredith 2007: 171)

The quotation contains all the ingredients of the national myth that undergirded the identity of the Afrikaner. Let us look at some of its component parts. As far as Afrikaners were concerned, again just as the Israelites of old, the "trek" was their Exodus. In the Jewish and Christian Scriptures, the Jewish people relate that they were slaves in Egypt, a foreign country where they came to live when, in a period of their history, they were weak and hungry. They went there from their country of Palestine because of a severe famine that struck the land. At the time of their arrival in Egypt and in the initial period of their settlement there, they were a privileged lot because of the position of their brother Joseph who invited them there. At the height of his fame, he had been given a high office that wielded a lot of power in the government of the Pharaoh. After the death of Joseph, the Egyptian kings who did not know the history of the Hebrews came to power. The situation of the Hebrews changed for the worse. They were viewed as aliens and subjected to forced labor as a result of which they suffered immensely. In the course of time, one of their ranks who grew up in the palace of the Pharaoh managed to secure their release. Moses led them out of the land of slavery into what was referred to as the Promised Land.

This travel from Egypt through the desert and the Red Sea (Sea of Reeds) to the Promised Land was their Exodus (*The Holy Bible* 1946; Robinson 1990: 273–275; 840–842; Hinson 1990: 45–85; Dobson 2002; Ceresko 1992: 72–79). It was viewed as a very defining moment in their lives as a people. In fact, they see it as the key event that created them as a people. Therefore, they celebrated it every year in an elaborate and solemn ceremony. In their view, it was the key moment that established them as a special and unique community.

The various key elements of the story of the Israelite Exodus are appropriated by the Afrikaners. In a similar vein, the latter harbored a very bitter memory of their oppression under the British. To escape from it, they moved away from the "land of oppression" that was life under the British. The "trek," the painful trip toward the north was their Exodus proper. In their move to an unknown land, they were faced with what they saw as great hardships. The Afrikaners further believed that the "trek" was inspired and led by God. They believed that God had entered a compact with them and brought them to their destination. Henceforth, throughout their history, this day became a special day, the day of the Covenant. They remembered the oppression, the journey through the dangerous territory and the settlement in the land. Once they achieved victory over their enemies, they erected a monument to their God.

Once the Israelites reached the Promised Land, they were ordered by their God to keep themselves pure by not mixing with the local population. There are different versions of the story here (Compare the narratives in the books of Exodus and Judges, Chapter 1). As related by one narrative of the "occupation," the story was more complex. This version relates that, at the initial stage, the Israelites were not as strong as the locals. Therefore, they infiltrated them slowly and began to cohabit, intermarry, and coexist with them. In contrast, the dominant narrative related that there was no room for the two, the new and the old, to live together. They were too different from one another to coexist. Therefore, the Israelites set about overpowering the indigenous populations. In many wars that were waged against them, the Israelites exterminated their opponents and seized their land. Consequently, the land became an exclusive reserve of the special people and their God.

In this same spirit and religious conviction, the Afrikaners moved in anywhere they fancied and dispossessed the local populations in South Africa from their land. The South African theologian Simon Maimela puts it as follows:

> It is against the background of the Afrikaners' understanding of their divine calling that apartheid was formulated and carried out. Theology was used to underpin this ideology; it was argued that God has sharply divided human races and the Afrikaner's calling was to help attain this goal of permanent separation, thereby preventing the admixture of races that would destroy "Western civilization" and the "God-given" identity of the white race. (Maimela 1994: 44)

Religion was the driving force that shaped politics. The wars waged against the other peoples (later the *Kaffir*—infidel, irreligious) was thus a "holy war" against the infidels. As the holy warriors continued in the pursuit of what they saw as their divine mission, the question of being declared infidels themselves loomed large and began to haunt them both from within and from without.

To begin with, the Dutch Reformed Church (NGK) held firmly on the doctrine of separate development and provided the religious arguments in its favor. The policy of separate development (the segregation of the races) was a point of discussion and resolution as far back as 1829. But it was in 1857 that the NGK resolved unequivocally that "segregation should be permitted. Support for segregation and apartheid within the Afrikaans Reformed churches developed into an involved ideology in subsequent decades, culminating in the 1974 report of the NGK...which provided explicit biblical and theological legitimation of apartheid" (Villa-Vicencio 1988: 145; 2002: 44). The leadership on all levels of life, even the political leadership, was also imbued with such a religious conviction that informed the politics of the day. Politicians saw themselves as instruments of God on a divine mission.

Consequently, "the Boer took a refuge in his church and his secret societies such as the Broederbond (literally, association of bothers), and he waited for the political power which would enable him to build a nation, where everyone was of the same mind, the same color, the same faith" (Lamb 1987: 326). The members of the "brotherhood" came from all walks of life. They were very prominent in their fields of practice. "From the beginning, the Bond included many ministers and teachers of religion. There is evidence, too, that the Broederbond sometimes attempted to tell the NGK members what to do at church meetings. Indeed, it was quasi-religious mystique that bound theologians, intellectuals, and politicians together in this peculiar brotherhood" (Hope and Young 1983: 30–31). The church's interpretation of the relevant texts of the Scriptures offered the strong theological base for the political system in vogue. The political pundits and leaders of the Apartheid era were members of this exclusive church. It was the faith expounded and firmly held in this church that gave the political class the conviction that underpinned their politics. Religion and politics were thus intertwined.

Gradually, however, the seemingly seamless argument began to unravel at one stage. Questions were being asked about the very basis of the system of Apartheid. Consequently, the religious arena began to become a battlefield. The interpretation of the theological basis of Apartheid became a bone of contention. The very church that was the staunch-est expositor of the system was rocked from within. The once united house that stood firmly behind Apartheid was increasingly divided. The staunchest supporters of the status quo stood on one side.

The conflict of opinion within the church intensified because of the emergence of another view that was challenging the official posi-tion. The proponents of this challenge were no longer satisfied with the belief that Apartheid was in conformity with the faith of the Universal Christian Church. They argued that Apartheid did not have its basis on the Christian Scriptures as its proponents claimed. On the contrary, it contradicted the true faith. This group increasingly became a vocif-erous opposition that questioned the very foundation of the system of Apartheid and the faith that allegedly supported it.

In the beginning, they were few. Naturally, they were branded trai-tors by the mainstream of the NGK because of the fact that some of the questioners had been related to the political establishment. One of the most prominent members was Dr. Bayers Naude, "South Africa's most prominent Afrikaner Christian dissident" (Billheimer 1989: 205). He founded an institution that forced a rethinking of the theological prem-ise that underpinned Apartheid and race relations. He went further and broke new ground by involving not only whites but blacks as well in the process of rethinking. He was also involved in setting up commissions to study the issue. He was later forced out of the church as a consequence of his public positions and activities against Apartheid. He was considered an apostate and barred from the membership of the church.

Another powerful attack against apartheid from within the Reformed Church family came from the black churches in 1981. They parted ways from their white counterparts and made a pithy declaration that rever-berated throughout the Christian world. In their opinion, they declared "Apartheid is a heresy!" In religious parlance, this meant that on the basis of the basic tenets of the Christian Faith, the policy and ideology of Apartheid contradicted the Christian Faith. It could thus not be called "Christian" in the best sense of the word. A strong voice was that of the (colored) pastor Alan Boesak. "By 1983, Boesak was becoming one of the most prominent anti-apartheid voices of the South African church, particularly internation-ally. The previous year he had been elected president of the World Alliance of Reformed Churches (WARC) at a meeting that isolated the White NGK by declaring apartheid a heresy…He was a powerful preacher; some people likened him, as an orator, to Martin Luther King, Jr." (Allen 2006: 205).

The religious battle was not confined to the NGK. Prominent religious leaders in South Africa such as the Anglican Archbishop Desmond Tutu and the Rev. Frank Chikane of the Apostolic Faith Mission entered the fray. They were vehemently opposed to the system and condemned it in very harsh and uncompromising terms. Through their various activities and think tanks, they critiqued the Apartheid ideology and attacked it relentlessly on the basis of the very Scriptures on which Apartheid was apparently founded. They used theological arguments to render it a tenet that contradicted the Christian faith. In this connection, the opinion of Archbishop Tutu was typical:

> From a theological and scriptural base, I will demonstrate that apartheid, separate development or whatever it is called is evil, totally and without remainder, that it is unchristian and unbiblical...If anyone were to show me that apartheid is biblical or Christian, I have said before and I reiterate now, that I would burn my Bible and cease to be a Christian. (Allen 2006: 198)

Following their footsteps, the South African Council of Churches (SACC), which brought together many churches in the country, also lent its support to the affirmation and subsequent resolution in 1982 that condemned Apartheid on the basis of the Christian Scriptures (Villa-Vicencio and De Gruchy 1983: 145).

INTERNATIONAL DIMENSION OF THE DEBATE

The assault was not confined to the internal debate only. The local proponents of this new wave of rebellion in theological thinking caught the attention of the outside world. One of the most interesting aspects of the discussion was that the issue became international as well. It was no longer confined to the country and considered an issue that concerned only South African Christians. Christian churches in many countries and many Christian theologians around the world pitched in to express their views on Apartheid and its religious foundations. World-wide Christian organizations such as the Geneva-based World Council of Churches (WCC) also came out forcefully against the allegedly Christian basis of Apartheid. In fact, they took a very radical step (Allen 2006: 213).

The WCC was however not satisfied with denouncing the evils of Apartheid and exposing its apostasy; it went further. It launched the Programme to Combat Racism (PCR) to fight against all forms of racism, not only in South Africa, but everywhere in the world where it manifested itself (Sjollema 2002: 935–937: 346–361; Tesfai 1996:140). Through this programme, it offered financial aid to support the humanitarian activities of liberation movements especially in southern Africa. Naturally enough, this move proved to be controversial. Many in the Christian community accused the WCC of supporting Marxist and Communist groups. The WCC stood firm. As a result, the battle lines between Christians were drawn sharply. The public square was engulfed in a heated debate.

On their part, the worldwide body of the Reformed Churches picked up and owned the declaration that "apartheid is a heresy." Not only did they declare it a heresy, but they went further when they resolved "to suspend the membership of the NGK and NHK (two white churches in South Africa) until such time as they stopped providing theological justification for the policy of apartheid." In the long run, the assault became so powerful and effective that the supporters of Apartheid could not withstand it. The churches' involvement had paid in the long run. In the opinion of one writer, "there can be little doubt that the Church played a key role in the ending of apartheid" (De Gruchy 1995: 211). The holy warriors were declared infidels and the edifice of Apartheid collapsed.

CHAPTER 2

RELIGION AND POLITICAL DIFFERENCES IN THE NORTH

IN THE PREVIOUS CHAPTER, WE SAW HOW THE RELIGIONIZATION OF politics had led to a very disastrous social and political predicament. Fundamental religious beliefs formed the basis of politics. Consequently, the religious faith that was based on the exclusion of the other created a political ideology that condoned and fortified the separation of human beings from one another on the basis of the color of their skin. Divisions of human beings based on race and ethnic origin became the norm. Religion built walls that divided the human family into a set of races that should be segregated from one another. At the end, fortunately for Apartheid, the internal and external forces stacked against it, including the religious ones that belonged to the same family, declared it untenable and contributed to its fall.

It is instructive to note that the mistakes committed by the system of religion-based Apartheid were to be repeated in another part of sub-Saharan Africa. Many ingredients of the systems in both places, namely South Africa and Sudan, are hauntingly similar. Even though two different religions are involved in both countries, the results proved, alas, disastrous for the populations in both cases. Different dominant societies far removed from each other by geography and religion evolved similar systems that led to catastrophes for the people concerned, especially the victims.

A number of writers have drawn parallels between the systems that operated in the south and the north of the subcontinent, namely, South

Africa and Sudan (Berkeley 2001: 218–219; Mugambi and Getui 2004: 24). On his part, Francis Deng states the similarity as follows:

> The Sudan has much in common with South Africa under apartheid, although discrimination expressed itself in strikingly different ways. In South Africa, apartheid excludes non-Whites. In the Sudan, Arabism both excludes, in the sense that it discriminates against those who are not Arabized or Islamized, and includes, in the sense that it fosters assimilation, which condescendingly implies rejection of or disregard for the non-Arab and non-Muslim elements. (Deng 1995: 14)

The similarity of both systems is not confined to the separation of the races that Apartheid imposed on the society. It goes further. One may be justified in saying that just as the system of Apartheid was based on religious convictions, so did the system that would prevail in the Sudan. The other war that took place in the northern tip of sub-Saharan Africa had also a religious thrust (Nyama 2000: 87).

THE MAHDI

There are differences of opinion as to when this religious outlook took root or consolidated itself in Sudan. Some go so far as to say that the religious factor had always been present in the politics and government of the Sudan ever since the Mahdi rose up against the Turko-Egyptian condominium (1882–1885). Islam became a rallying cry against those that were viewed as outsiders and infidels. It galvanized the population through a messianic leadership. There were a variety of themes that were important and coalesced in the rise and activities of the Mahdi. They are encapsulated in the names the Mahdi used to refer to himself: "The Imam, the Successor of the Apostle of God, the Expected Mahdi. As the Imam, he asserted his headship of the community of true Muslims. As Successor of the Apostle of God, he envisaged himself recapitulating the role of the Prophet, by restoring the community which Muhammad had established. As the Expected Mahdi, he was an eschatological figure whose advent foreshadowed the end of the age" (Holt and Daly 1988: 87).

On the one hand, there was a nationalistic fervor. The Mahdi and his followers were bent on chasing out the foreigners who had taken control of Sudan. The Mahdi and his followers were thus engaged in what could be called a nationalistic project. On the other hand, however, there was a far more important religious side to the Mahdi. He was the embodiment of a pure Islam. Perceived as "the Imam, the successor of the Apostle of God and the Expected Mahdi, the divine leader chosen by God at the end of time to fill the earth with justice and equity," he rolled into one all the attributes of a respected and true leader in the eyes of his followers. In such a capacity, he is seen as having made enormous contributions in both the religious and national spheres in Sudan. In fact, the religious and national (political) aspects were not separated from each other (Holt and Daly 1988: 87, 97).

The religious factor at this time was a sort of a two-edged sword for both the north and the south. On the one hand, the Muslim north was often involved in the slave trade. There was of course a racial side to this exchange in slaves. On the other hand, at least initially, many from the south also saw Islam as a possible way to liberation from their situation of slavery. The understanding was that Muslims only enslaved those who are considered unbelievers. If one became a Muslim, one would be emancipated because it was against the law to enslave a fellow believer. In fact, there is an example from the early history of Islam: "The fact that the first Muezzin (caller-to-prayer) appointed by Muhammad himself was Bilal, the Abbysian [sic] slave (who was freed on becoming a Muslim), was and continues to be a profound source of inspiration, for Blacks can proudly say: 'There is no more shame in this Blackness'" (Mandivenga 1991:82). Once converted, the new believer belonged to the worldwide Muslim community. As a member of this community, one is spared from bad treatment, such as slavery. Once the individual or group adopt the Muslim faith, they are spared from the wrath of enslavers.

This of course was not to be. The racial factor prevailed and eclipsed most of the benefits that may have accrued from the adoption of the new religion by the potential slaves. Some of the believers even went so far as to say that the Islamization of the south was resisted on the basis of the idea that if the slaves converted to Islam in their droves, their area would eventually cease to be "the land of war." The lucrative institution of slavery would thus cease to be justified.

Be that as it may, according to various observers, there are many factors that conspire as it were to pit the north and south in bitter wars (Ali, Elbadawi, and El-Batahani 2005: 193–220; Ali and Elbadawi 2005: 143–161). In terms of physical confrontation, the first war was ignited in 1955. When one considers the reason behind the uprising of the south against the north, one finds that one factor stands out among others. The issue of religion has played a very significant and even predominant role. Such an idea is not necessarily shared by all and sundry (Badal 2006: 1–14). There are also those who provide a more nuanced explanation (Hasan and Gray 2002: 96).

Mohammed Salih on his part argues that this is a simplistic explanation (Salih 2003: 96–120). He notes that religious differences are not the only factors that divide the north and the south. First, when one looks at the south, it has many differences that pit its own inhabitants against one another. Because of these differences, the people are engaged in clashes among themselves. One reason that easily comes to mind is that of ethnicity. The Nuer and the Dinka, to name just two, have had their share of differences and have involved themselves in violent conflicts. The most consequential was the split within the SPLM/A between the forces of Garang and Machar that took place in 1991 and led to much bloodshed. It had no religious connotation at all because they both belonged in the same religious camp. Questions of political and personal ambitions as well as ethnic elements certainly played their role. The same may be said in the case of the so-called Muslim north. The conflicts that are raging in the Dar-Fur and the east have nothing to do exclusively with religion. All the inhabitants of these areas are Muslims themselves. They have grievances that pit them against the central government in Khartoum.

But there are those who differ. As far back as 1994, the late Dr. John Garang de Mabior, the then leader of the SPLM/A, had clearly stated that religion and racism were at the center of the revolt of the south against the north. In a speech delivered at a convention of the movement held in south Sudan in 1994, he accused what he referred to as "the ruling social group that has been ruling our country,... popularly known as the 'Jellaba' as being behind the war and the destruction that ensued in the country." He said that this group had the twin objectives of imposing a racial and religious superiority over the rest of the population. In his own words, he stated it as follows:

> The tragedy of the "Jellaba" as a social group is their narrow Arabo-Islamic outlook and their total failure to look beyond these two parameters of Arabism and Islamism as the sole uniting factors for the Sudan. (Garang)

According to Mohammed Salih, such an analysis was a result of reflection that was developed later. The original political orientation of the manifesto of the SPLM/A was socialist through and through. It did not reflect or include any religious inclination. It called for a "new Sudan" where religion or creed would not be dominant. In these early days of the military movement, this political orientation often posed as a counterpart to the wishes and activities of the churches in the south. In the long run, however, the SPLM/A was pressured by the churches in the south to modify its course. The pressure was also applied in reaction to the stringent religious line that was being followed and applied by the government in Khartoum. In the course of time, there was an increased rapprochement between the churches and the SPLM/A. They even began to reflect each other's positions in the name of the interests of the south and its people (Salih 2003: 110).

Be that as it may, according to some other observers, religion and ethnicity had often been used as instruments by various governments in the history of Sudan. Such instrumentalization of religion in politics had a long history stretching back to the introduction of Islam in the country and the invasion of Arab peoples of the area. We had also seen how the Mahdi married religion and politics in carrying out his campaign. Perhaps in line with this precedent and tradition, the independence of the Sudan from Britain in 1956 introduced a marked emphasis in the policies and politics of the governments that exercised power in the country. In line with Garang's thinking, Francis Deng observed, "Since independence, ruthless attempts to dominate, Islamize and Arabize the South have characterized the process of successive governments" (Deng 1995: 11, 36; Waihenya 2006: 56; Johnson 2003: 35).

NIMEIRI AND SHARIA

It seems that the first overt attempt to use religion as a political instrument in post-independence Sudan was carried out by Gaafar El Nimeiri. When he took over power in a coup in May 1969 (referred to as the "May Revolution"), he had relied more on progressive and even leftist elements of the Sudanese parties and society. The communists and other secular-oriented individuals played a very central role in his seizure of power. It was with their support that he led the coup. He emphasized the secular nature of the state. Under his leadership, the Sudan was even named "The Democratic Republic of the Sudan." To substantiate such a move, he included many elements that were more inclined to lean to the left of the political divide. There were even southerners in what was called the

Revolutionary Command Council that led the country. The leadership also included communists, which seemed to wield some power in the political direction the government was taking.

It was such a secular orientation that had contributed to a decisive step to address the "southern problem." Nimeiri brought a fresh input into the equation. He was even instrumental in the signing of the Addis Ababa Agreement in 1972 between the southern Anyanya I movement and the government. The movement was founded to fight against a number of measures that were taken by the government to promote and accelerate the process of Islamization and Arabization. Many Christian missionary institutions such as schools were forcibly closed and missionaries expelled. Friday became the day of rest. These measures, among others, fuelled the revolt.

President Nimeiri had embarked on taking a variety of measures that watered down the agreement and even contributed to its virtual abrogation (Khalil 2002: 58–71). He decentralized the administration by redrawing the provincial boundaries in the south.

At the same time, the red flag of Islam was raised openly. In 1983, Nimeiri undertook the most drastic measure, which, by all accounts, was a watershed: he declared that, henceforth, Sudan would be governed on the basis of the *Sharia*.

Such a proclamation shook the southerners to the core. They had often hoped and fought for a political system that recognized their political and religious rights. They were counting on the establishment of a secular system that would reorganize the political situation in Sudan without reference to religion. The new move by Nimeiri suddenly abrogated the agreements to which they held. The agreements had been worked meticulously and were witnessed by external groups. This time round, Nimeiri took a unilateral decision that did not take into consideration the will of the southerners. For all these reasons, "the north/south conflict has become a religious conflict" (O'Fahey 1995: 39, 42; Nyama 2000: 34; Holt and Daly 1988: 204).

This religious direction taken by the Nimeiri regime had very far-reaching consequences for Sudan (An-Na'im 2003: 37). With this proclamation, religion had assumed the upper hand and defined politics. The inevitable consequence was that the unilateral decision pitted the followers of the Muslim faith in the north against the followers of the Christian and traditional religions in the south. The war had now assumed a clear religious tone. In the past, religion was not totally out of the picture.

Now, it came into the open and took center stage. Consequently, both sides began to harden their stances. In their arguments regarding the defense of their positions, religion came to play a very important and significant role.

NIF AND JIHAD

Two years after the proclamation, the regime of Nimeiri was toppled. Some political activity where political parties began to play a role was revived. However, this did not last long. The religious position hardened once again after the coming of the Al-Bashir regime in 1989. The field was now free for the open advocacy of the Islamic dispensation in the political arena. With the coming into the scene of Dr. Hassan Al-Turabi, and his alliance with the military takeover, religion and politics were married to one another indissolubly. Al-Turabi, the leader of the new party in power, the National Islamic Front (NIF), was the guiding ideologue of the regime that took over. Meredith describes the man as follows:

> His (Al-Bashir's) guide and mentor in this enterprise was Hassan al-Turabi, founder of the National Islamic Front (NIF) and head of the Muslim Brotherhood, who had played a prominent role in promoting Islamist ideology during Nimeiri's regime earlier in the 1980s. A diminutive man, with a white wisp of a beard, educated at universities in England and France, bespectacled, erudite and charming, he saw himself at the centre of an Islamic revival that would transform not only Sudan but other countries in the region. An Islamic scholar of world renown, he represented the genteel face of Bashir's totalitarian rule. (Meredith 2005: 588; Berkeley 2001: 195–202)

The ideology of the NIF was manifestly Islamic. From this vantage point, President Omar Al-Bashir addressed enemies both within and without. First, on the local scene, there were two potential opponents: "He is a true Islamist, as his frequent calls to 'jihad' against internal opposition testify. The biggest threat to Islamists is the opposition of ordinary Muslims, and the NIF's first targets after the 1989 coup were the northern Muslim opposition." Second, a little further from the center, the south with its rebels also posed as a religious issue. "The south is still an Islamist cause...In November (2008)...Omer called on the Popular Defence Force 'mujaheedin' to mobilize for 'jihad' again."

Third, external forces beyond the Sudan consisting of adherents of other religions are the next target. Their opposition to his rule is seen through a religious lens. "He repeatedly attacks 'infidels' and Jews, and presents opposition to his regime's ethnic cleansing programme in Darfur as a Jewish and Christian plot." In this divided world, he is possessed with the fiery conviction that it is a fight between right and wrong in the religious arena. "Western nations have no ethics or morals. And we will export it to them...We are strong with our values and we are waiting on Allah's promise to obliterate them."

Overall, the project of Al-Bashir is unequivocal. It is a pristine and classic example of the religionization of politics. Al-Bashir does not mince his words in this regard: "We are here to emphasize the Islamisation of the state. There was a great deal of secularism and we want more Islamisation."[1] With firm religious convictions, not only did the regime aim at changing the face of the Sudan but had the temerity to expand its influence and control on the African continent as well, a sentiment expressed by Sadiq al-Mahdi in 1966 (El-Batahani 2001: 163; Hasan and Gray 2002: 37). Henceforth, the religious direction of politics was open for all to see. The language was consistently and openly religious: even *Jihad* became the leading vocabulary (Sidahmed 2002: 89).

The lines were thus drawn as sharply as they could. Henceforth, a number of steps were taken to instill the idea of *Jihad* on the populace. First, the Popular Defense Forces (PDF), which was a mere military outfit when it was established in 1989, was transformed. It was formed into *Mujahidin,* "holy warriors." These fighters were no longer a regular army to defend a government and people but an army with a religious mission to defend the faith and the land. Second, the transformation of the fighting force was accompanied by intense countrywide propaganda. Third, committees were formed in various parts of the country to promote and strengthen the new outfit. The aim of the committees was to disseminate the information and aim of the force and to garner the support of the population. In some areas, special financial contributions were made to further its aims. Businessmen were asked to make special contributions for the cause. The committees would also be instrumental in mobilizing the society to increase recruitment. Organizations were created to care for the fighters and their families. Fourth, the members of the force were indoctrinated when they joined it. Special lecturers were assigned to them to teach them on the new faith-based defense and its goals. One account provides some details:

> PDF serves as instrument of religious indoctrination and militarization of
> the Sudanese society... The whole program is imbued with religious mil-
> itancy. The overall premise is that the trainees are aspirant mujahedeen
> who must make the sacrifices required by that status. Lecturers [who are
> mostly political cadres of the NIF] teach that Sudan is a pioneer Islamic
> state, threatened by a hostile world. PDF are intended to throw fear and
> disorientation in the hearts of the infidels and enemies of Islam, recruits
> are told. The rebels of southern Sudan are depicted as outlaws and agents
> of the enemies of the Islamic state and the faith, who have to be fought in
> a holy, total war, according to lecturers.[2]

The role of the media was important in this religious mobilization. It glori-
fied the fighters and the wars they conducted. Letters written from the war
front that described heroic exploits by the holy warriors became a staple of
the media. Stories of young people who left everything behind and died in
the defense of the cause were broadcast with great fervor. The pressure on
the parents was also relentless. They were called upon to encourage their
children to volunteer accepting what was depicted as a sacred calling. The
fighters on their part were presented as defenders of the faith and the land.
They were also elevated as martyrs. As such, they were promised direct entry
to paradise with all its benefits, including the much desired virgin wives.
Organizations that supported the martyrs and their families mushroomed.

The PDF fighters were drawn from all walks of life. Civil servants,
teachers, and students were eligible for recruitment. The youth were a special target. They were naturally courted more than any other members of
society. When the need arose, when the numbers of the forces dwindled or
the wars in the south became intense, the government reverted to rounding
up people from the streets. Occasionally, some recruits were taken against
their will and sent to the war front. The PDF was also used in suppressing
any opposition activities in the north. However, the bulk of the fighters
were dispatched to the south. They took part in the war against the rebel
forces such as the SPLM/A that was fighting the government. Many of
these unfortunate young people perished in these hapless wars.

In this religious divide, it was not only non-Muslims in the south
who were alienated from the north. This also affected the Muslims in
the south. Any Muslim who was in one way or another associated with
or participated in the war on the side of the south was also regarded as
being outside the Muslim faith, an apostate. Once the war was viewed in
religious terms, all those who had a hand in the conflict were divided on

religious grounds. A *fatwa* (excommunication) was promulgated in 1992 by religious scholars against any Muslim who stood on the side of the struggle in the south. "An insurgent who was previously a Muslim is now an apostate; and a non-Muslim is a non-believer standing as a bulwark against the spread of Islam; and Islam has granted the freedom of killing both of them." The consequences were tragic. "The 'freedom of killing' involved slaughter in the south on a massive scale...PDF units and government-sponsored militias massacred civilians and plundered their property and cattle at will. Thousands of women and children were captured as war booty and forced into slavery" (Yousif 2006: 48; Meredith 2005: 593).

JIHAD AND INTERNATIONAL OUTREACH

As stated earlier, at the center of it all was the mercurial Hassan al-Turabi. He was interested not only in Sudan; he had an international project. On the home front, he was the ideological mastermind of the regime that took over in 1989. On the international level, however, Al-Turabi was convinced that there was no turning point in the march of Islam to dominate the world. He was of the opinion that Islam is the wave of the future that is posed to conquer the world. "Islam is a new force that is going to come anyway, because it is a wave of history. It represents modernity in Islamic societies. It will come through evolution if it's allowed to come peacefully and gradually," he is quoted as saying (O'Brien 1995: 215).

As a result of such an ideological certitude, Sudan was increasingly becoming the nerve center of a religious movement with global ambitions. All forces inspired by Islam wherever they may be found were welcomed and coordinated from this center. Increasingly, this center gave way to militant Islam that espoused violence to reach its goal. Islamic militant groups from Algeria, Egypt, and Tunisia as well as the Palestinian rebel leader, Abu Nidal, well-known for his bombing of foreign targets and the Palestinian Islamist group, Hamas, were welcomed. Groups that opposed systems that do not reflect the Islamic constitution based on *Sharia* were embraced as constituent members of the movement (Berkeley 2001: 196). It is in this atmosphere that Osama bin Laden found refuge in the Sudan. In the words of Meredith:

> Among those who chose Sudan as a convenient new abode was the wealthy son of a Saudi construction magnate, Osama bin Laden, inspired,

like Turabi, by the ideas of establishing an "Islamist International." For ten years, bin Laden had been involved in the jihad against the Soviet occupation of Afghanistan, first as fundraiser in Saudi Arabia and the Middle East, then as an organizer based in Peshawar on the Pakistan border. Together with a Palestinian academic, Abdullah Azzam, he established the *Maktab al-Khidamat* or Afghan Service Bureau, overseeing the recruitment and training of foreign *mujahidin* (guerilla fighters)...Bin Laden was generous with his support for Turabi's pan-Islamic ambitions...He was equally active in organizing insurgent networks...Sudan had provided him with an invaluable opportunity to incubate terrorist networks over a period of five years and to position his own group, al-Qa'eda, at the centre of jihadi activity. (2005: 591–593)

In the course of time, cracks began to appear between the two central figures in the country, Al-Bashir and Al-Turabi. Ever since the former took over power, they had become the inseparable couple. They both supported each other by holding military and ideological power respectively. In the event, they were not able to continue together. The reactions from the outside world, including the neighboring countries and the West, were proving to be too much. They accused each other of deviating from their original religious aims. In the power struggle that ensued, Al-Bashir moved against his erstwhile comrade and imprisoned Al-Turabi. Even though the latter was pushed out of the pact, the religious line that was forcefully represented by him, namely, the *jihadist* mission of implementing strict and pure Islam was not abandoned but reenforced further.

In a way, the prominence of religion and the hardening of its proponents may eventually have contributed to bringing the warring parties in the north and the south—the NIF government and the SPLM/A—to the negotiating table. The war attracted a lot of international attention. The Christian-Muslim dichotomy in the conflict finally drew powerful groups to have a significant interest that may have changed the situation on the ground. There is no question that, among these groups, the interest and powerful lobby of Christian fundamentalists in the United States had significantly influenced the Bush administration to seek a lasting solution to the war in Sudan. In the end, in a strange twist, the factor that had earlier contributed to the escalation of the war, namely religion, became one of the main factors in its resolution. Again in a strange twist, followers of the two religions were shouting religious slogans in the same parliament building as they celebrated the adoption of the new constitution that was approved after the signing of the peace agreement in January 2005:

> Sudan's National Assembly today unanimously passed a new constitution...Amid shouts of "Allahu akbar", or God is great and "hallelujah, hallelujah!" the 286 lawmakers who attended the session stood with their hands in the air to pass the constitution.[3]

Considering the bitterness of the past caused by religious views, one is bound to ask: Is this an anomaly or a taste of the future? Will religion also play a unifying role and become an instrument of peace as it had earlier been an instrument of war? It is a question that should be pursued and which cannot be neglected.

THE MISSING DEBATE

The case of South Africa showed that there were serious debates from within and without on the policy of Apartheid. Many Christian believers and religious leaders contributed their share to the discussion. There were protagonists who represented the arguments for and against Apartheid. In a way, it was a massive involvement by all kinds of people who took their faith seriously. However, in the end, the result proved constructive. People had a stake in the correct interpretation of the Faith they adhered to. The debate in the public square was by all accounts edifying and refreshing and geared toward the solution of a faith-instigated and faith-based system or line of action.

The chapter began by noting the similarities between the cases of South Africa and Sudan. They involved both religion and race. The only difference was that the perpetrators of racism in South Africa were whites while those in the Sudan claim to be Arabs. The tragic fact is that there was lack of serious debate in the latter case, both internal and external. As we shall see in the last chapter, there was only limited discussion. It has yet to contribute to a wave that would make a difference.

In the south, one must admit that the churches were in the forefront of the debate. They contributed to it through their meetings, writings, and advocacy work. They reached out to the wider world through what were called ecumenical relations. Many of their international counterparts picked up their concerns and became closely involved in the debate. As we shall see in chapter 7, there were some attempts toward this direction.

On the whole, however, African and Arab "solidarity" proved too power-ful in the end. In most cases, this entailed the determination not to wash one's dirt in the open or not to betray Afro-Arab "brotherhood" in the face of a supposedly bigger and greater enemy, usually, the West. Such reticence and perception succeeded in stifling the debate that could have contributed to a solution.

On the one hand, in the majority of cases, Africans (both Arabs and blacks) in the continent, found it embarrassing to criticize one of their own. They shied away from pointing out the wrongs that contributed to the conflicts that destroyed the lives of many people. They preferred to look away as the tragedy played itself out in the public arena. Only a few dared raise their voices in a situation dominated by what could only be referred to as a conspiracy of silence. It seems that a tacit consensus prevails by those who count, especially those in places of leadership on many levels, not to condemn or criticize one of their own. In the face of such a gaping silence—not only about the case in Sudan but also in many areas of conflict in the continent—there are only a few voices cry-ing in the wilderness. The sad fact is that no one would pick up such cries and comments and carry them forward so that they may become waves in the public square.

In this connection, one quotation stands out by its capacity to inter-twine very effectively the many potential protagonists that should have initiated and taken part in the debate. In the process, the participants in such a debate would have advocated a different world than the one that has perpetrated and continued a condition of untrammeled tragedy. Even though some of the points contained in the following lengthy quo-tation may be debatable—one could entertain a different perspective— the uncharacteristically bold and courageous naming of the potential protagonists by the distinguished Kenyan Professor Makau Mutua is singular and rarely paralleled:

> Shockingly, the African Union (AU) has impotently sat by, unable to do anything meaningful, including calling the barbaric killings geno-cide. The conflict pits the Sudanese government and the Arab Janjaweed militias, on the one hand, and black Africans on the other...It is a cam-paign of ethnic cleansing...Equally shocking has been the complete silence about the genocide in the Arab and Muslim capitals of the world, especially in Africa and the Middle East. Those Arabs and Muslims who shout the loudest against the repression of Palestinians by Israelis have refused to raise their voices and condemn the killing of black people in

Darfur. The tragedy of Darfur demonstrates that the fundamental fault line in Sudan is race, not religion, although the latter added fuel to the fire in the south...The Darfur conflict follows the familiar pattern of the government's war against its own citizens in the south. President Omar Bashir and his fundamentalist Islamic government declared a "holy war" against African groups in the south—the Dinka, Nuba and Nuer peoples...Khartoum's genocidal policy in the south, just like in Darfur, was an evil grab for resources...As a first step, the AU must end the hypocrisy in Afro-Arab relations. Sudan, the bridge between black Africa and Arab Africa, should lead in rewriting the historical script between the two peoples...What kind of brotherhood does the AU practice if Arab states will not stand up and force Sudan to end the killing fields? There is even talk that Mr. Bashir wants to be the chairman of the AU. How can a known perpetrator of genocide head the continent's premier good-governance body? (Mutua 2006: 32)

Prof. Mutua lists the potential actors and issues that should be involved in making a difference and influencing the debate for the better. First in the list is the African Union (AU). There have been complaints from many sides that it has not been in the forefront of finding a solution to the problems of Sudan. The only time that it came close to sanctioning the government was when it bulked from naming President Al-Bashir the chairperson of the AU after the summit held in Khartoum in 2006. Even though there have been calls for tougher actions from many quarters, President Al-Bashir has argued that the problem was an African problem that should be solved by Africans. His counterparts seemed to have acquiesced to this line of argument. Sudan resisted by playing successfully the African card. The resultant stalemate showed that Africans were not ready to bring the issue into the public arena and argue the cases for and against the critical issues that served as the sources of the war, including religion and race. Criticisms of the AU were not lacking on this score.

The second actors that are mentioned by Prof. Mutua are the Arabs. They are close to Sudan because of their religion, Islam, and "race." They could potentially play a significant role in addressing the crisis. They all adhere to the notion that they belong in the "Arab nation" and are members of the Arab League. Sudan also claims to be part and parcel of the Arab/Muslim world. At the same time, some of the Arabs/Muslims also form part of North Africa and are members of the AU. In the light of these intertwining factors, it could be said that they possess a significant potential to influence or impact the situation for the better.

Lack of the adequate use of this potential has led to accusations that the Arab/Muslim world has not done its best in contributing to the resolution of the crisis in Sudan. As a matter of fact, there are indications that they have not been evenhanded in addressing the crisis in Sudan and other issues closer to their hearts. While the Arabs protest about the plight of the Palestinians in the hands of the Israelis, Prof. Mutua argues, they choose to do comparatively little about what is happening in Sudan. In many cases, one notices that other actors are blamed for any action they do or do not take. For instance, "Western imperialism" and their allegedly colonial designs on Sudan are routinely mentioned as negative intentions by the international community. The argument of Colonel Gadaffi in this connection is telling:

> Libyan leader Muammar Gaddafi accused the West today of trying to grab Sudan's oil wealth with it's plan to send UN troops to Darfur and urged Khartoum to reject them. "To be occupied by the Sudanese army is better than to be occupied by the UN forces, and the biggest disaster is if the Atlantic army came and positioned itself in Sudan..." he said. (Reuters 2006: 14)

Even so, concerns about the absence of the Arab/Muslim contribution to the debate and to a possible solution to the crisis in Sudan continue to be asked. This is the case with the point raised by the head of Amnesty International:

> Arabs have been asked to show "the same urgency and energy" in calling for the protection of civilians in Darfur as they have shown toward Lebanese and Palestinians. "Arab public opinion needs to wake up to this issue," Amnesty's Secretary General Irene Khan said of the humanitarian crisis in Western Sudan. "They cannot be concerned about the human rights problems of Muslims and other groups in the (Palestinian) occupied territories and Lebanon and turn a blind eye or remain silent in the face of what's happening to Muslims in Darfur..." Protests in the Arab world in July and August during fighting between Hezbollah guerillas and Israel attracted thousands of people concerned for the welfare of Lebanese civilians. (Reuters 2006: 18)

The point is that narrow religious, nationalistic, tribal, racial, or ethnic boundaries should not close one's eyes to the plight of others who are different in these categories. It is imperative to consider the suffering of other people who are not considered one's own. If this is not done and if the discriminatory attitudes continue unabated and unaddressed, the violent conflicts that beset these areas will not subside. They will also cause greater conflagrations that will have serious implications for the regions concerned and beyond.

Prof. Mutua further mentions the issue of race in the configuration of the conflicts. As had been mentioned earlier, this factor is playing out menacingly in the fault line that divides the Arab north and the African south. A number of countries are now being adversely affected by this phenomenon. Beginning from Sudan, other countries such as Chad, Niger, Mali, Mauritania, and even Senegal are affected by some unfortunate developments related to this issue. The interethnic and interracial conflicts are inflamed across geographical and national boundaries. The most conspicuous conflicts in this category are affecting Sudan and Chad. Ethnic and racial groups from one country are sucked into and entangled in the conflicts of the other. The issues of race and ethnicity thus become potential powder kegs that destabilize entire areas (Oshidari and Bamezon 2007: 15).

The most disturbing element is that "Arabs" and "Africans" are fighting it out in very inhospitable environments. The tragedy is that people who had been living together peacefully for years are killing one another. By all accounts, the future is bleak in terms of coexistence. The landscape is being changed for ever. New alignments are taking place that threaten the future for a long time to come (Sanders 2007: 14).

This racial and ethnic configuration that is taking place in this region has far-reaching consequences. Taking this fact into consideration, Prof. Mutua rightly challenges the so-called Afro-Arab brotherhood. Considering the fact that the government of Sudan is protected in all possible ways, he wonders aloud whether such a thing as Afro/Arab solidarity exists in the light of the Arab (re)action or its absence in the situation in Sudan. If the high ideals of such a close relationship are to be realized, as they must be for the benefit of the two peoples, some changes have to take place. Both entities must find joint mechanisms to address the plight of the victims and assist in finding lasting solutions. It is heartening to note that there are voices even from the Arab world that are arguing this line of thinking. Such is the case by the Arabic newspaper published in London, the *Al Hayat* (Hasbani 2007: 34).

The final issue that ties all things together is religion. Whatever the variegated problems facing the Sudan, the question of religion is prominent. One cannot avoid the conclusion that, whether by design or by default, religion has become a very potent instrument in casting a very thick shadow over the many strands of life. The following of the government and the NIF cannot be held together without the appeal to religion. Those who support the continuation of the conflict whatever its cost are doing so because of the religious conviction that informs their political actions. The young recruits to the militias and the army are attracted by the appeals to a *Jihad*, "holy war" against infidels. It is the call to defend the faith and the land against alleged "unbelievers" who belong to the "land of war." Ultimately, it is a religious project carried out in the name of God. This religious mission colors all activities. It could also play an important role in the search for solutions.

CHAPTER 3

RELIGION AND VIOLENT CONFLICTS IN THE WEST

WEST AFRICA HAS HAD ITS SHARE OF VIOLENT CONFLICTS. The most destructive and tragic wars were the ones fought in Liberia and Sierra Leone. The two countries had become like twins as the victims of the war that engulfed them. Both were dragged into war one after the other. The war that started in Liberia did not leave Sierra Leone alone. Rather it became an extension of the war. As a result, neither of them was able to extricate itself from the destructive consequences of the conflict alone. The problem was that, as geographical neighbors, and through the leaders of their respective rebellions, their fates were tied together. The leaders of the two rebellions also saw to it that they helped one another in their quest for power (Meredith 2005: 545–573). The human and material resources of one were used to bolster the insurgency of the other. For example, Charles Taylor of Liberia was heavily involved in the mayhem that had gripped Sierra Leone. Taylor also coordinated his activities with those of Foday Sankoh who led a vicious rebel group, Revolutionary United Front (RUF), in Sierra Leone. As the two countries were tied in war, their escape from war also depended on each other. They also dragged other neighboring countries such as Nigeria, Ivory Coast, Burkina Faso, and Libya in to the war.

Violent conflicts also affected two other countries in the region: Nigeria and Ivory Coast. In what follows, each area of violent conflict is discussed with an eye on the prevalence and prominence of the religious component.

Liberia

From the start, the political system that was established in Liberia was a special one (Sanneh 1983: 53–105). It was created and led by approximately 300 families of freed slaves who came from the United States of America to settle on the coast of West Africa in the first half of the nineteenth century. They established a republic in 1847. In a sense, the so-called Americo-Liberians established a system that was not far removed from the system of Apartheid that obtained in South Africa. Even though they were of the same color as the ones whose land they settled in, they saw themselves as a people apart. The indigenous peoples who owned the land before them were considered primitive in their view. Therefore, as a civilized people, they saw it as their right to look down on them and treat them as second-class citizens. In the course of time, they evolved an administrative structure that gave them the upper hand. They gradually imposed themselves as the undisputed masters of the land. The political game of leadership was restricted to their small and tightly knit constituency. The latter evolved into a separate and distinctive clan vis-à-vis the ethnic groups who were already settled there. Consequently, the leadership only changed hands among the numerically few settlers and their descendants (Meredith 2005: 546).

Religion, in this case Christianity, was at the heart of the governance system in Liberia. This did not prevent the elite from being members of secret societies. Neither did it prevent them from appropriating relevant aspects of African Traditional Religion. "Successive presidents of Liberia have had themselves proclaimed leaders of the influential Poro male initiation society. William Tolbert, president of Liberia from 1971 to 1980, was both supreme *zo* of the Poro society and president of the World Baptist Alliance" (Ellis and Ter Haar 2004: 79). The public face of the religion of the state was Christianity. On the whole, religion was interwoven into the way the country was run. As a public statement that religion and politics did not separate, the last leader of the country, President William Tolbert, was a minister of the Baptist Church. His vice president was the head of the Methodist Church while the leader of the main party (True Whig Party) lead the Presbyterian Church, "an example of total fusion of church and political leadership" (Haynes 1996: 48). Consequently, religion played a central role in the running of the country. Church and state were closely related to one another and supported each other (Sanneh 1983: 105). Religion was so dominant that it is even accused of having contributed to the destruction of the country by covering up the many injustices that festered for years (Salih 2001: 54).

The doomsday of the system came in the beginning of the eighties. The government of President William Tolbert was overthrown by one of his very own bodyguards, a twenty-eight-year-old army sergeant called Samuel Doe, an "indigenous Liberian." His team of disgruntled officers overpowered the loyal guards who manned the presidential mansion and killed the president. In a violent orgy that would henceforth mark the Liberian civil war that ensued, President Tolbert was murdered in cold blood. His body was mutilated and buried in a common grave. From this moment on, not only did Liberia start the road to self-destruction; it also dragged the adjacent region into turmoil (Ellis 1998: 164–167).

Religion was never far from the war. Most of the people who kept the war going had always expressed religious sentiments:

> Many of the main protagonists in the war have claimed, some with obvious sincerity, to have been in direct communication with God at various stages of their bloody careers. This is not just a personal quirk, but is situated in a history in which religious belief has functioned as a mainstay of political and social orders... "Halleluiah!" Prince Johnson declared as he harangued a group of frightened civilians shortly after Doe's murder. "Yes! I killed Doe through the power of God... I killed plenty of people that day right here at Freeport here. Praise the Lord!"... Samuel Doe himself, for example, believed strongly that something or some force he identified as God... was directing his fate, like the voices heard by Joan of Arc and many another heroine or hero of old. (Ellis 1999: 23–25)

Both Traditional African Religions and Christian convictions held by the parties in war heavily contributed to the war effort. In fact, one cannot separate the religions from one another. They were all mixed up to produce what was believed to be the most effective religious concoction to determine the course of the war. There were no clear boundaries that stood between the religions. From the perspective of the African Traditional Religions, there were those who believed that some potions and postures were important in the art of warfare. They believed that they helped the armies to have the upper hand over their enemies. Through the potions that they used, they also instilled fear into the hearts of their enemies.

Leaders such as Samuel Doe had their own "spiritual advisers" who gave them counsel on the spiritual aspects that allegedly overpowered the deadly effects of physical armaments. Consequently, Doe was feared both in life and in death. When he was alive, he boasted that no bullet had been manufactured that would kill him. In this way, he sowed terror on his enemies who believed his supposedly miraculous prowess in defying death. On their part, his opponents were also terrified of him. When they killed him and disposed of him, they still believed that he had the exceptional powers in him to influence the course of Liberian politics. In other words, they believed that he was detrimental to Liberian politics even from his grave. Therefore, his grave was dug and his remains cremated. There were also special priests who served the aims of war. They involved themselves in a variety of rituals that consisted of killings, both human and animal, and using body parts in creating potent concoctions. Some consisted of drinking blood or eating fetus and so on (Richburg 1998: 134).

A testament by a former "priest" from Liberia, one called Blahyi, is revealing in this regard. His testimony throws an interesting light into the manipulative spiritual practices that were an integral part of the art of war:

> And so at the age of 11, Blahyi was officially crowned the priest of the community...He became the key personality in black magic...As the war broke out towards the end of the 1980s after the macabre killing of President Samuel Doe...Blahyi was to climb to the peak...taking charge of the spiritual element of the warfare that pitted them mostly against Charles Taylor's government forces...Blahyi claims that through black magic, he was able to "programme" fighters to become killer machines, but as the war intensified, he also moved to the frontlines and would personally take the lead in penetrating enemy lines, naked (thus his *nom de guerre* General Butt-Naked who led a group referred to as the Naked Base Commandos of the Krahn) but with a gun and ready for mental warfare... "The agreement was that I had to make a human sacrifice to appease the gods. That is how the dread of me started." (Wamari 2008: 2, 3)

Never were the combatants devoid of religious sentiments. In their war efforts and their survival mechanisms, they often referred to and submitted themselves in their own way to higher and supernatural authorities. Prince Johnson was the one who ambushed Samuel Doe and tortured and killed him. On his part, his religious sentiments were expressed when he would often break into singing Christian hymns in the midst of moments characterized by violent orgies of torture and killings. At the end of his ill-fated adventure as a rebel and after committing innumerable atrocities during his rebel days, he even went to Nigeria to study Christian theology and become a preacher. Even Blahyi went to Israel, reverted to Christianity, and is heading a church of his own.

At this stage, it would also be in order to inject the story of Sierra Leone and its war not least to provide a background to the peace process that contributed to the end of the war, which will be dealt with in the final chapter. As has already been indicated, the two wars were extensions of each other (Adebajo 2004: 167–188).

The first connection was the one cemented between Taylor of Liberia and Sankoh, a former army corporal, of Sierra Leone. In the first place, their meeting in Libya in 1988 and their training in the country became the basis of their future relationship. They were both trained and supported by Libya before they ventured into their respective territories. Second, the rebels in Sierra Leone were heavily influenced by the tactics of the Liberian rebels under Taylor. They copied their strategies and applied them in their contexts. Third, fighters from Liberia were supporting those in Sierra Leone. Those in Liberia also swelled their ranks by recruiting Sierra Leonean exiles in Liberia and sending them across the border. Finally, the natural resources of Sierra Leone were exploited to the maximum and used in the war through the intimate collaboration of Taylor and Sankoh. The rebel leader in Sierra Leone and Taylor worked hand in hand to extract the maximum benefit in their war efforts. They used the massive resources of Sierra Leone, especially the so-called blood diamonds, to their own advantage.

Beginning from the first president of the country, Siaka Stevens, the seizure of power meant the use of the diamond mines for one's personal enrichment. Everybody knew that diamonds were the heart of Sierra Leone. This knowledge did not escape Sankoh and Taylor. They were convinced that if they are to finance their war efforts, they had to get hold of the diamond mines of the country. In 1991, Taylor financed a contingent of fighters of the RUF lead by Sankoh. Taylor dispatched them across the border and took over the diamond fields (Meredith 2005: 572).

Once the wars were over, the financing of wars through ill-gotten wealth from natural resources had to stop. Diamonds could no longer circulate as before. They had to be bought and sold with a certification, which proved that they were mined legally. The UN had instituted the Kimberley (after the South African city, so-called diamond capital of the world) Process that subjected the sale and purchase of diamonds to a strict regime.

The fact is that material advantage and wealth were foremost in the conduct of the war. There were also a number of immediate causes that form the basis of the war in Sierra Leone. In the first place, before the war, the country was run on a patrimonial basis. There were no bureaucratic institutions in place that saw to it that the resources of the country were distributed equitably. The elites in power at any given time simply shared the economic and political spoils in a way they saw fit. The system held together as long as there were enough resources to go around that served to mollify a great number of people. The system of patronage encountered serious problems once the resources dwindled especially due to the change in the international political and economic order. It could no longer meet the demands of the population. In the event, some parts of the country began to distance themselves from the center. The control the center had on them began to loosen. The areas inevitably fell into the embrace of rogue elements that seemed to offer a more lucrative way. The influence of the Liberian civil war was decisive in this context. Rebel contingents crossed over and created connections that proved devastating to the country in the long run. Consequently conflicts became the order of the day.

Second, there was another more decisive factor. The youth population had swollen disproportionately. Beginning from the seventies, the number of disgruntled youth began to grow. Many of these youth were not reached by services that should have been offered to them by the state. The educational service, to name but just one, was not adequate enough to meet the needs of the young population. Many students dropped out of the educational system. Even those who completed their education could not find jobs. Many were thus left to their own devise. With time in their hands, they were left to fend for themselves. They formed groups and clubs that nursed their wounds together. In the course of time, their grievances were exploited by would-be revolutionaries that came their way. Such a volatile youth population was a ready recruiting base for people like Sankoh.

The war began in 1991 and lasted up to 2002. It was extremely harsh. While the group that started the rebellion continued in its own way, others also splintered from it. In the course of time, there were numerous groups that fought for supremacy. All aimed their rebellion at seizing power from the government of the day. The rebel groups sustained themselves by resorting to illegal and illicit mining of diamonds. Worst of all, they became notorious for the means they used to control the population. For instance, to prevent the farmers from harvesting their rice, they resorted to cutting the hands of village women. By extension, they also had the intention of instilling fear into the hearts of young people who abandoned the rebel movement because of hunger. Once there was no food to return to, the rebel leaders reasoned, the escapees would have nowhere to go. The terrorized fighters would have no choice but to remain in the rebel camp, hungry or not. In other words, the logic of the amputations lay in the deterrence of the youth from abandoning the war effort.

As the rebellion grew, its brutality was not confined to the way it treated civilians. Even its treatment of its combatants was equally brutal. It brooked no opposition. It also terrorized all those who fell under its jurisdiction. Its reasoning was that it would only control strictly those who fell under it by instilling fear in them. Many were thus abducted, integrated into its ranks against their will, and tortured. Executions and mutilations became a way of life. One of the odd practices of the RUF was the tattooing or marking permanently of recruits (such as slaves of old) so as to prevent them from escaping. Once marked in this conspicuous way, the combatants had nowhere to hide. Even if they succeeded to run away, anyone would single them out as former guerillas and subject them to punishment. They were also controlled very strictly through a system of passes without which they could not move from one place to another. Only the possession of permits or passes allowed them to move around. Anyone caught without a pass would be arrested and subjected to all kinds of punishment and even death. The recruits were thus confined to camps that were kept under strict surveillance.

There were no winners in the war except the rebels. Consequently, it continued unabated. There were several attempts to bring the fighting groups together and bring about a peaceful resolution to the conflict. The various factions that led the government and the rebel groups could not agree on any common platform. In the process, out of the 4 million inhabitants of the country, approximately 30,000 civilians had been killed and approximately 40 percent of the population displaced.

Religious conviction was prominent in the two wars. Taylor was the one who took the religious argument to what could be called its logical conclusion. He put the various convictions that manifested themselves in the other rebel leaders into a sharper perspective. To begin with, like all the others, he was an adept at religion. Being a Christian did not prevent him from practicing African Traditional Religions as was the case with many other leaders in many African countries, a complicity he shared with his comrade-in-arms, Sankoh. "Taylor shared with the late Sierra Leonean warlord Foday Sankoh the services of a *juju* man, Alhaji Kuyateh...At the same time, Taylor claims to be a born-again Christian. He prayed together with former US President Jimmy Carter and regularly welcomed American preachers to Monrovia" (Ellis and Ter Haar 2004: 79).

To be effective in war, Taylor claimed God on his side. By doing so, he reflects and summarizes in a forceful way the positions held by the various warring parties regarding their views of the wars they perpetrated. None of them, it seems, would fight without claiming to have God's support. The war that Taylor was waging, as far as he was concerned, was a "Christian holy war" in which the Christian God of Taylor's conviction was heavily involved. In the war that Taylor waged, the first protagonist was God. The people who fought were only carrying out the plan of God that had already been laid down from above. All these holy warriors under such an enlightened leader with a divine inspiration were only instruments of a higher command. In the expressed opinion of Mr. Taylor, the holy warriors in his entourage beginning with him as their head were only functioning as tools in the grand scheme of things. They had simply subjected themselves to the divine will. First among them was Taylor himself.

As was noted earlier, such a spiritual worldview was not confined to Taylor alone. It imbued the population of Liberia as well. They had the firm belief that a divine power has so much dominance over the people and nation that they had no choice but to be subject to it. The people become the instruments of this power and wait for any outcome whatever their participation and role in it:

> Since Liberia is a land created by God—so the reasoning goes—and is under God's protection, politicians and others can engage in the most blatantly self-interested behaviour and ignore the long-term implications of their actions, since everything is in the safe hand of the Almighty. (Ellis 1999: 257)

As is evident in the question and answer session (see the quotation at the beginning of the book), the claim to be God's holy warrior and on the side of God is not accepted readily by all. As posed by French, there is a very serious question that accompanies the conviction by the leader who claims to be in cohort with and an instrument of God. The possibility of being an infidel looms large just at the border of the conviction of the holy warrior. The ambiguity is stark clear. It is one that will hover over anyone who conducts war and violence that claims divine inspiration and basis. In the case of Taylor, even though the theological argument did not continue in the open and was never resolved with the authority it deserves, at the end, he was removed from power. The earthly authorities were too much for the holy warrior who claimed to be God's tool. First, they forced him out of office. They then banished him from his country. He became a refugee temporarily in another country. Continuing their pursuit of him, they arrested him and extradited him to The Hague to the chambers of the International Criminal Court (ICC) to face earthly justice. These measures, coupled with the election of the new president, Ellen Johnson-Sirleaf, brought about the end of the war. There are still loopholes here and there as the president herself acknowledged (Johnson-Sirleaf 2007: 11). In the judicial process, the infidel side of the holy warrior was exposed to the world, not by a tribunal of a theological judgment, but by the instruments of human justice.

There is another tragic side to this saga. The fact is that the question posed by French was not treated with the seriousness it deserves even by religious authorities. It was not pursued relentlessly to find a plausible answer by all those who should concern themselves with such weighty matters that relate violent conflicts and religion. The theological side of the war and its consequences were not treated adequately and did not find a solution. To do so, a process such as the one which dealt with the issue of Apartheid would have been in order. Unfortunately, that was not the case. One has the inkling that, in the absence of a serious debate in the public square of this very issue, one very important aspect and cause of the war has not been addressed and put to rest. One of the very significant sources that created and sustained the war was not settled to the satisfaction of all concerned.

Since the religious issue was at the center of the war, a forum should have been made available to give it a final resolution. Since this was not the case, the question of the religious side of the war must be turning and churning in its shallow grave. It needs to be dug out, viewed for what it is, analyzed, settled, and comfortably reburied, at least, for the foreseeable future. Even if, as is the nature of theological issues, the debate cannot be settled once and for all, it could offer an important healing process. It could even offer some guidelines to possible wars—in light of the fragility and possible "return to conflict" the current president refers to—that might erupt in the future claiming religious convictions. In any event, dealing with all aspects of the war, including the religious, is extremely appropriate to definitely end the war that had caused so much destruction and trauma.

In Liberia, there is a persistent feeling that the war had a lot to do with the spiritual world. Many people are convinced that Liberia has to come to terms with the spiritual aspect of its life. Some of them are offering what they think are solutions to the crisis. Others are not so sure (Paye-Layleh 2006: 16). On the whole, there is no consensus on the analysis of the problem and the possible solutions. There is no doubt that many are groping toward addressing the issue in their own way. How much they will succeed in their groping is anybody's guess. One may say that unless this aspect of the life of Liberians is addressed adequately and to the satisfaction of many concerned, there will remain a vacuum that might prove threatening in the long run.

NIGERIA

There is much evidence to show that violence took place in various parts of Nigeria especially after independence. Many of them were sparked by religious reasons and strengthened by religious affiliations. The conflicts pitted various religious groups against one another. This was one aspect of the holy warrior/infidel divide that rocked a greater part of West Africa. This time round, it was a war that spawned a religious divide between Christians and Muslims. It had also an intra-Muslim aspect. There are those who argue that the seeds of such a conflict were sown as far back as the colonial beginnings (Gofwen 2004). On the whole, Britain, the colonial power, did not tamper with Islamic institutions that had been in place at its arrival. The Pax-Britanica that was imposed also accorded Muslims enough space to exercise their religion freely and to expand without any restrictions.

Even in this period, it does not mean that Islam was a unity. It also harbored divisions within itself that contributed to occasional internecine conflicts. In part, this had something to do with the various traditions that resided within Islam. These traditions were partly represented by the brotherhoods of *Qadiriyya* and *Tijaniyya*. On the one side, the former consisted in a tradition that could accommodate itself to all kinds of governments, whatever their origin. This included even the British who were ostensibly Christian. On the other side, there was the latter that espoused a *Jihadi* tradition that hibernated in the background. Even though this tradition did not always erupt in violence, it persisted to hold sway among the leadership. These two streams were not the only manifestations of Islam. There were also other undercurrents that opposed the influence of the colonial power.

As is also the case in some other countries in sub-Saharan Africa, one observes that these serious divisions within Islam in Nigeria have difficulties in coexisting with one another. The various parties even go so far as to accuse each other of being heretical. Some religious practices of one are rejected or viewed as flouting the norms of the faith by the other. Consequently, the various tendencies within the religion clash once in a while. Violent confrontations have taken place among Muslims as well going back to the 1950s. These were instigated more or less by different and incompatible interpretations of the faith. Other reasons consisted of the use of mosques by one or the other faction, the call to establish an Islamic state, Mahdist tendencies which denounce society for its apparent ills and call for its purification even through violent means.

A more recent cleavage is the one between the Sunni and the Shia. In the process, mosques are destroyed, some religious leaders, ordinary believers and policemen are also killed. Some brotherhoods fight against each other. Some of these confrontations stretch over a long period, causing a great deal of harm. In some cases, the intra-Muslim violence pauses as a serious threat and challenge to the state apparatus. The story of the Maitatsine sect carries all these ingredients.

> The Maitatsine sect can be traced back to the 1950s when Marwa, a minimally educated convert to Islam, posed as a Koranic teacher in Kano and in that capacity began challenging the basic tenets of Islam, particularly the legitimacy of Mohammed as the final prophet of Islam...Posing as a Koranic teacher provided Marwa with the opportunity to form a rebel force...who received magic charms to "preserve them from bullets" and were taught to trivialize death. (Zinn 2005: 102)

Over and above these important intramural disagreements, there were numerous other sources of tension on the Nigerian scene. In light of the post-independence history, one could say that the most important of them all was religion. For instance, in the wake of independence, there was an atmosphere of mistrust between the Muslim north—the so-called Islamic emirates—and the Christian and African Traditional religious south. Both sides were vying for and unsure of who would wield power once the British left (Miles 2000: 212). They were jostling to seize the reins of power. Consequently, the history of Nigeria is interspersed with violent conflicts that had their source in such a religious divide.

At one point, two issues that had originated from the Muslim side became causes for violent conflicts. They were the membership of Nigeria in the Organization of Islamic Conference (OIC) and the introduction of *Sharia* in the north. Membership in the OIC was made public in 1986. The sudden announcement created uproar within Christian circles. Violent conflicts broke in opposition to it and fifteen people died in one incident. Such conflicts also arose when the north argued that a provision to have a federal *Sharia* court be included in the national constitution. A majority of Christians opposed the idea. The tension generated by such a proposal threatened to tear the country apart on religious lines.

On many occasions, one also witnesses the fact that the government leadership on the national level often tilted one way or the other. They were perceived to have either favored or promoted to power members of one religion at the expense of the other. For instance, a leader may give the necessary permit to the Muslim side for the construction of a mosque. At the same time, Christians may be refused a permit to start educational establishments. Some leaders may also be disposed to bring more Christians into the government and the military. With religious tensions in the background, it always proved difficult to strike the right balance. Suspicions are nurtured on all sides; they often became causes for clashes.

Religion becomes an explosive mix when it is tied to ethnicity. During elections, political parties connected to different ethnic groups play a leading role. A false step on the part of one or the other party creates tensions that erupt into clashes. In many instances, ethnic and religious rivalries and subsequent conflicts arise especially due to the failure of a government to provide basic services. As a result, many ethnic groups rise up against those they see were benefiting from the government as a consequence of holding important positions of power allegedly due to their religious affiliations. Under such conditions, federal and regional government positions become battle grounds for control by different ethnic and religious groups.

BIAFRA WAR

One is reminded of the Igbo persecution and massacres in the north in the 1960s. Following a coup in 1966 by an Igbo Christian, the north reacted with suspicion and a feeling of fear of dominance. When the coup leader, General Ironsi promulgated a law stating that the federal government had been abolished and that state civil service jobs would henceforth be based on merit, the reaction was swift. The Igbo became the immediate target because they were Christians and more educated in contrast to the Hausa of the north. The latter were suspicious that the former would take all the lucrative jobs offered by the government. The reaction to the promulgation led to the death of thousands of Igbo living in the north. Once again, a few months later, approximately 30,000 Igbo perished in further massacres. This eventually led to the flight of approximately a million Igbo to their area of origin in the southeast. It was followed by the Igbo attempt to form an independent state of their own. The declaration of independence came on July 6, 1967.

At first, the reason for the proclamation of an independent homeland was couched in political and economic terms. It was argued by its proponents that it was in search of security for the Igbo. At the same time, it aimed at taking over the resources of the region for its own benefit, especially oil. As time passed and the war intensified, however, the predominantly Roman Catholic Igbo began to convey their struggle in religious terms:

> On the Biafran side Christian ideas and images were crucial in the war propaganda. The war was presented as a battle between the "Christian nation" of Biafra and the Muslims of northern Nigeria who launched a *jihad* against the Igbo, and this image was employed systematically in the effort to create sympathy for Biafra in the West. (Kastfelt 2005: 3)

The whole exercise that lasted for approximately two and a half years led to the death of approximately a million Igbo (Banjo 2003: 88–103). Religion also did play a prominent role even though the ethnic card was also prominent in this tragedy. Both ethnic origins and religious affiliations had a place in the conflict. Once the war was over and the ill-fated leader of the rebellion, Chukweumeka Odumegwu Ojukwu, saved his skin by fleeing to Ivory Coast, there was a manifestation of magnanimity especially from the head of state of greater Nigeria. General Yakubu

Gowon, a Christian from the north, had seized power through a coup in 1966 that toppled General Ironsi. He was in turn overthrown in 1975 while he was attending an OAU meeting in Uganda. While in power, he took a number of measures to heal the wounds of the Biafra war. A generous spirit of reconciliation brought the two sides together; the tension subsided. Many Igbo went back north as a result of this reunion. Ironically enough, the reasons for antagonism moved north to erupt once again at a later date with a vengeance.

As subsequent history also shows, there were religious issues that became sources of conflict in other parts of the country (Meredith 2005: 585–587). The *Sharia* debate was in the limelight in the years between 1977 and 1978. It has increasingly become a source of contention ever since, ostensibly in the north. This trend where religion becomes a major source of conflict picks up especially after the 1980s. Various seemingly mundane reasons fuel the conflicts. Construction project of a church building in proximity to a mosque, for instance, gave rise to Muslim anger. A seemingly simple quarrel between students in 1987 led to the burning and destruction of churches and mosques. Many people also died in the process as a result of these violent conflicts. The possible arrival of a Christian preacher from abroad becomes a cause of violent conflicts in 1991. In view of such violent irruptions, the future of Christian-Muslim relations and its effect on the country becomes an issue of major concern.

For instance, after the election of General Olusegun Obasanjo in 1999, to just refer to one example, the Yoruba felt short-changed by his election, even though he himself was a Yoruba. In their minds he was just being used by northern Muslims. Many of the Yoruba did not vote for him. Their hero, Chief Abiola, a Yoruba tycoon, had won the presidential election held in 1993. However, General Sani Abacha refused to give up the post of presidency that he had assumed through a *coup*. Instead, he imprisoned Abiola who eventually died in prison in 1998. Bitter for the loss they felt after the death of Abiola, the Yorubas vented their anger by clashing with their Hausa counterparts. Their life together was shattered suddenly. Once the Yoruba began to attack the Hausa, the latter fled to what they considered their own region, namely, the north. In turn, once the Hausa reached there and the news of their persecution spread, it was their turn to attack the Yoruba in their midst. Such inter Yoruba and Hausa clashes replicated in other areas where they used to live together in harmony.

Again since 1999, there were some disturbances that rocked some states of the Nigerian Federal Government. The incident that provoked the anger of the Christians in many states was the announcement by a governor to declare *Sharia* as the law that governs the northern state of Zamfara (Sani 2008: 9). The Christians who lived in the state as a minority were outraged by the move. This was not all. Twelve other states followed the decision to impose *Sharia*. The outrage over this move extended farther. States with Christian majorities in the south threatened to retaliate by proclaiming their states exclusively "Christian." In this connection, Meredith writes,

> A Christian protest in the city of Kaduna in February 2000 resulted in bloody clashes leaving hundreds dead. Entire neighbourhoods were "religiously cleansed." Many of the victims were Igbo. In revenge, Igbo vigilante groups in southern Nigeria killed hundreds of Hausa migrants from the north living there. As thousands of refugees and emigrants fled from the far north, religious tensions increased in other areas. Jos, the capital of the Plateau State, hitherto renowned for its peace and quiet, was engulfed in clashes between Christian and Muslim groups in 2001 in which 3,000 died. (2005: 587)

Initially, there were clashes in the three North Central states of Bauchi, Kaduna, and Kano in 2000 and 2001. The violent conflicts were caused by a mixture of factors that somehow managed to ignite the confrontations. One cannot ignore the fact that there were ethnic and land issues that contributed to the clashes. There were grievances here and there that were based on ethnicity and economic factors. One of the sensitive issues that arose in this connection was that of "indigenous" versus "settler" groups. There were many people who came to some of these areas from other states be it in search of work, business opportunities, or better life due to urbanization and increased mobility. These so-called settlers often vie for resources with the local communities or indigenous inhabitants of the areas. In some cases, they may even succeed far beyond the indigenous groups. They would then be resented. Grudges accumulate toward "foreigners or settlers" viewed as invading and expropriating the land, which is considered to belong solely to the locals. Unfortunately, such emphases on differences are not confined to Nigeria alone but manifest themselves far and wide, sadly and tragically, in many parts of sub-Saharan Africa (Ellis and Ter Haar 2004: 106). Such a polarized situation only needs a false move by one party or another to lead to a conflagration that engulfs a given area.

In such a situation, it is often taken for granted that each ethnic group has an area from which it originates and to which it has intrinsic rights. All the rights and privileges thus accrue to the particular ethnic group. Anyone who comes from another state to live and work in such a state will always be regarded as a foreigner or a migrant. Any rights that one might have may thus be challenged or stripped bare at any given moment for any apparent reason. Ethnic origins thus assume a great significance in the distribution and maintenance of rights, be they economic or social. The separation among people of different ethnic origins casts a shadow on whatever one undertakes in any given state. In some places, no one is accepted or integrated in a community other than the one to which one belongs. In some of the cities, the areas are separated among various communities who have not crossed artificial borders. Some parts are occupied by Muslims while others are occupied by Christians. And, sometimes, the two never seem to meet and build bridges.

Once these underlining differences are inflated for one reason or another, they are further strengthened and rendered explosive by ethnic-religious factors. In many cases, while one ethnic group belongs to one religion the other belongs to a different one. It follows then that in the same state, in this case, the Plateau state, to just mention one example, the Muslim are Hausa-Fulani while the Christians belong to the Gamai ethnic group. It happened that in the first months of 2004, the Muslim Hausa-Fulani attacked the Christian Gamai ethnic group. Many people died in the attack. Much property was also destroyed. For some time after the initial attack, the confrontation seemed to die down. The Christian Gamai had abandoned their homes and fled. But not for long! They were only biding time to regroup and prepare for a counterattack.

At another given moment, they struck back! The Christian Gamai attacked their Muslim counterparts and created havoc in the city of Yelwa in the Plateau state. They surrounded their enemies in an early morning raid. The enemies were taken by surprise; there was no route for escape. The premeditated attack had not given them the chance to prepare and resist the assault. The city was razed to the ground; many people died in the process. The city had lost its life. Most of the people had no choice but to abandon it. Their livelihoods were shattered and the future seemed to have no prospects at all. Many of those who survived the vicious attacks were thus forced to pack up the small possessions that they had left and abandon the city.

The same story of mayhem and destruction is told about another city—Kano. There was peaceful coexistence in the city. Muslims occupied the central part of the walled city. Many others who did not belong to it were also permitted to come and live and trade in it. There was no question about the fact that people had devised ways and means of living together and sharing life without facing any serious problems. In this and other similar cases, it seemed that there were no insurmountable challenges that stood in their way of interacting with one another even in the face of differences. Exchanges of all kinds were taking place without any sort of difficulties.

Suddenly, however, a whole way of life is swept aside in a flash of anger. A violent conflict caught up with everyone without any warning that gave people time to prepare for the worst that was to come. As sudden as it came, the conflict destroyed everything in its wake; no one was spared. Both the perpetrators and the victims were caught up in a spiral of violence. Friends and those who interacted well with each other for years could no longer see one another in the light of the past. Worse still, conflicts that had taken place in one area had triggered conflicts in other areas. The conflict that took place in Yelwa in the Plateau State fed the one that came later to Kano City in Kano State. Muslims and Christians clashed mercilessly. Once revenge killings take place, there is no way to stop them; they create and sustain their own momentum (Odunfa 2004: 23–27). Lives of many innocent people were destroyed beyond repair. Many women and children were abducted and taken away by rival factions.

More confrontations on religious basis have taken place recently. When one studies these clashes, one sees that they throw some light on why they take place and what triggers them. In the first place, some of them are based on events taking place outside the country. For example, the publication of the cartoons on the Prophet Mohammed published in far away Denmark and other European countries provoked violent protests in the northern city of Maidugri. Muslims went to the streets to protest their publication. The protests that eventually became anti-Christian culminated in the destruction of many church buildings and businesses owned by Christians. As many as fifty people were beaten to death in the riots that ensued. There were retaliatory measures that also culminated in the death of Muslims and the burning of Mosques by Christians. Many Christians see such violence as a deliberate move by Moslems to turn Nigeria into a Muslim country. Strangely enough, clashes also take place between Christians and Muslims in support of Israel and the Palestinians respectively.

Second, two other northern cities, predominantly Muslim, were also set on fire. The cities of Katsina and Bauchi were hit. People were killed and churches burned. A reason that runs like a red thread through all these violent conflicts is that they are set in motion by leaders for their specific political ends. As one observer pointed out, "sectarian violence is often stoked by politicians seeking to bolster their own power bases."[1] Sadly enough, this observation is not confined to Nigeria alone.

Third, as we have mentioned earlier, the introduction of *Sharia* also becomes a trigger. "Religious violence has killed thousands since 12 northern states introduced Islamic law in 2000, alienating Christians."[2]

Fourth, some seemingly minor incidents give rise to violent reactions. An alleged desecration of the Muslim Holy Book in one school, for example, led to a rampage. That very mishap was the cause that gave rise to riots that spilled over into the streets of Bauchi.

Fifth, political discussions could also serve as sources of violent confrontations. There are continuing discussions on the constitution, which sometimes do not contribute to agreement on the matter. Even a planned meeting on the issue would become a cause for violent disagreements.

Sixth, further political issues such as the possibility of the change of the constitution enabling the former president of the country, Olusegun Obasanjo—who was a Christian—to run for a third term also become sources of violent reactions. At that point in time (2007), the Moslems in the North were of the opinion that two terms of a Christian president were enough. It is now the turn of one of their own, they argued.

Seventh, Christians and Muslims fight over the national census. Both sides want to assert that they are the majority in the country. The point that religion would not be included in the census is greeted with anger by some people on both sides of the religious divide. As a result of all these clashes, as the *Economist* magazine says, "around 20,000 have been killed in God's name since 1990, estimates Shehu Sani, local chronicler of religious violence" (2007: 3–22).

The conclusion on the basis of all these events is that religion plays a very significant role in the rise of violent conflicts. Unfortunately, their persistence casts a very disturbing shadow on the future of the country. Whether one admits it or not, it compromises the prospects of a peaceful future. The coexistence of religions poses as a serious challenge to the nation. The view of Miles in this connection is one that must be taken with great seriousness:

> Looking beyond the most recent return to civilian governance, we conclude by confirming not only the pluralities of Islam in northern Nigeria but the increasing salience of religion in the Nigerian polity. Religious resurgence—Christian as well as Islam—will continue to challenge not only the viability of democracy in Nigeria but the very relevance of Nigeria as a unified, secular and constitutionally based federal republic. Reconciling northern Islam to Nigerian democracy remains a formidable test in this much vaunted symbol of African nationhood. (Miles 2000: 221)

With this warning in mind, we continue our coverage of the West African states and the religion-based conflicts that affect them by turning to Ivory Coast. It presents us with the continuing saga where religion has also played a very important role in affecting the destiny of a nation.

IVORY COAST

To begin with, one notes that the Christian and Muslim population of the country is divided equally. On the whole, the policies and political orientation of the first head of state, Felix Houphouet-Boigny, tended to marginalize the Muslim part of the country. As a result, Muslims felt that they were treated as second-class citizens. They were more or less excluded from the machinery of the state. Still, they were not bereft of both economic and commercial clout. The president was not unaware of the danger paused by foreign influence that might affect the country's Muslims. With this in view, he was not devoid of taking intermittent steps to appease his Muslim constituencies. He even built two mosques, a big one in his hometown, the village of Yamoussoukro. He also organized a Muslim council on the national level. In the process, he wanted to have a handle on the increasingly assertive resurgent Islam and its implications for the country and his power. He even appointed a Muslim, Alassan Ouattara, as prime minister in his cabinet (Calderisi 2007: 115–30).

Problems were contained to the satisfaction of the leadership as long as the economic miracle was in vogue and the Big Man was alive. Once the economy began to deteriorate in the mid-eighties, however, opposition voices began to rear their heads even from the Muslim side. The people who became affected by the economic downturn, many of them prominent Muslims, turned against the government and became vocal opponents. The construction of a sumptuous basilica in the president's home village at the cost variously estimated from approximately $145–$400 million raised the eyebrows of the Muslim community. It was taken as a sign that the country was tilting toward becoming a Christian state at the expense of Muslims. Even though murmuring mounted and criticisms were surfacing, the Christian-Muslim relationship was often characterized by a spirit of tolerance.

The death of the first and only president since independence—Felix Houphouet-Boigny—unleashed negative forces that had been hiding under a cover of civility so far. In the first election, the two candidates who hailed from the two religious communities—Henry Konan Bedié, a Christian and Alassan Ouattara, a Muslim—sharpened the contradictions that had been gestating within the society. Bedié was in a hurry to assume power without biding his time. He could not wait for constitutional niceties that expected him to wait for a parliamentary decision. He made himself the interim president. His foremost desire was to outmaneuver Ouattara. The turn of events brought into the open the religious and ethnic cleavages between the south and the north.

Once Bedié had the power of the presidency in his own hands, he began to harass the followers of Ouattara. He went further. Muslims in general were also persecuted. While embarking on such actions, he had also secured the backing of a part of the Muslim leadership. Others among them were marginalized further. Many Muslim army officers and civil servants were dismissed. By attacking Muslims frontally, Bedié was becoming reckless. In his desire to consolidate power, he was contributing to the destruction of the national fabric by marginalizing openly one part of the society. The rights of anyone who looked like a Muslim were violated to the extent that their identity cards were torn by the police. It was clear that the policies of the Bedié government were aimed at making it clear to the Muslims that they did not belong in the country.

The straw that broke the camel's back had to do with the question of identity. Bedié promulgated a law that defined "the true Ivorian." According to the new law, anyone who aspired to that privilege had to be born from what were said to be "100 percent Ivorian parents." They should have also lived in the country for more than five years. The law was promulgated to target especially Ouattara and to disqualify him from running for an elected office, mainly the presidency. It was seen that Ouattara was born from parents who hailed from Burkina Faso. He had also lived many years outside the country. The implication was that the true Ivorian was only a Christian from the south. It was a step that led the country into a disastrous course.

In its heyday, Ivory Coast was the envy of neighboring countries. It had created an economic miracle that attracted millions of people from other countries (Lamb 1987: 212–219). At one point, a quarter of its estimated 8 million people were foreigners who benefited from the economic boom. They were attracted by the high incomes they earned in a variety of economic activities. The cocoa plantations not only served as the sources of foreign currency for the country but also supported many foreigners who worked in them. All in all, it was a bright spot in an otherwise bleak region. No wonder that its economic and political stability was unique in the area. Unfortunately, however, unbridled search for power and political expediency by the first president and his successors brought the country down.

Some Muslims still stuck it out with Bedié. Others became more vociferous in their opposition. The Muslim community was thus divided into the Bedié and Ouattara camps. Violence began to be used one against the other. Attempts were made to eliminate some leaders. In any case, the Ouattara camp argued that all the machinations of Bedié were aimed at dispossessing the Muslim community. The seeds of civil war were sown. It was only a question of time until the proponents of one or the other took up arms to make their point. Once that point was reached, the once prosperous country was plunged into an economic and political quagmire. Even the elections that followed could not return the country to normality. Instead, they exacerbated the situation further (Eluemunor 2008: 19).

In the 1980s, Laurent Gbagbo, a history professor at the University of Ivory Coast, was an opposition figure. Viewed as a progressive, Gbagbo often irked the president through his activities. He later became president in elections conducted under dubious circumstances. Once he gained power, he was not able to reverse the disastrous policies introduced by his predecessor Bedié. Instead, he pursued and deepened the religious chasm by using religion to consolidate his power base. As a result, the country descended further into chaos and division. The country was more and more divided on ethnic and religious lines. The predominantly Muslim north simply went its way. President Laurent Gbagbo on his part consistently used the religious card in his campaigns to maintain power. He had railed against non-Christians and foreigners. His xenophobia was aimed not only at immigrants from neighboring countries but against the Muslims in the north as well. From his side, Christian militias had been created to bolster his political programmes. In the opinion of one writer,

> Cote d'Ivoir's bout of instability, including the civil war that broke out in September 2002, is rooted in the exclusion of the Muslim opposition from the political system, accompanied by the enrolment of the Christian community into the army and the creation of Christian militias... Gbagbo has also mobilized Christians against Moslems... He has restructured the army through "the military enrolment of Christians loyal to him (Gbagbo)."[3]

It is also reported that, President Gbagbo's wife, who is said to wield a great deal of influence on the president and the country as a whole, claims to be a born-again Christian. Her convictions have a considerable influence in making policies and in the political arena (*Economist* 2004: 80). From her point of view, there was a clear division between those who were on the side of God and those on the opposite side. Those who were on the other side, namely, the Muslims, were on the wrong side of the political divide. This divide is described in religious terms. The separation was not only political but it had religious and spiritual basis. In fact, it can be described only in religious terms. "Simone Gbagbo had been breathing hellfire on the rebels in speeches delivered not just at political meetings, but also at evangelical churches. Madame Gbagbo has not been overcome by affection for the mainly Muslim rebels she has regularly accused of doing the devil's work... She believes her own and her husband's positions are divinely sanctioned."[4] As a result of this polarization, " the country is deeply divided over ethnicity and religion" (Polgreen 2006: 19).

Many peace agreements were tried since the civil war broke out. None was able to hold. Finally, an agreement brokered by one of the staunchest opponents of the Gbagbo regime succeeded in bringing the two parties together. Blaise Compaore of the neighboring state of Burkina Faso had often been suspected and accused of siding with the rebels. Nevertheless, the peace agreement he drew succeeded in bringing the belligerents together.

There are still a number of issues that have to be finalized before the country returns to a full fledged peace. Among the most sensitive and dangerous include disarmament, Ivorian identity, and presidential elections. One sees an important issue not being put on the table. As was the case with Liberia, one should point out that an issue underlying the civil war has once again been skirted. There is no question about the fact that religion had played and continues to play an important role in the events that unfolded. It should have been seen as an important component of the situation following the civil war. All concerned, including the religious leaders, have to address it in a manner that paves the way for a life together between the parties. Since it had become an issue and played a significant role in the division of society and causing havoc, only a frontal and concerted effort to deal with it can offer a lasting solution. The ambiguity of the holy warrior/infidel has not been resolved. It is biding its time.

CHAPTER 4

RELIGION AND SIMMERING VIOLENCE IN THE EAST

THE TWO COUNTRIES OF EAST AFRICA, Kenya and Tanzania, are homes to a sizable portion of adherents of Christianity and Islam. For the most part, they have been spared from experiencing violence caused by religious divides. There are numerous developments that witness to the fact that times are changing. The global and the local are impacting on these countries and pushing them to deal with the situation that is evolving rapidly. In the light of some recent developments, one wonders at this stage how long the status quo will withstand the pressures of a changing environment.

In one way or another, the global impact has brought both Kenya and Tanzania unexpectedly and inexorably into the limelight. In August 1998, the two countries became targets of unprecedented and hitherto unforeseen bomb attacks. The American embassies in Nairobi and Dar-es-Salaam were subjected to suicide bomb attacks that caused considerable human and material damage. The buildings were razed to the ground by powerful blasts. Many people died and many others were injured in the process. Even though the targets were the United States' embassies in the two countries, the bombings introduced a new dimension into the religious equation of the countries. They were sucked unwillingly into the religious confrontation that would determine the global scene in the years to come. Even Uganda was not spared from the consequences. The bombings had cast a shadow over it. Security concerns related to the bombings began to surface and take center stage. For Kenya and Tanzania, the repercussions were far-reaching indeed.

Aside from this incident, when one looks at the religious situation in both countries, one finds that there are some similarities and also some differences between the two countries . Uganda may also be included in this category. It is now time to look in a brief manner at the three countries that, together with Burundi and Rwanda, are members of the East African Community (EAC).

KENYA

It is interesting to note that religion has played an important role in the politics of Kenya. Significantly, it has colored the views that both people and politicians held on political developments. If one looks at the Muslim side to begin with, one notices that ever since the bells of independence began to ring, Muslims were divided in their expectations and wishes. Those who lived in parts of the country other than the Coast were generally throwing their lot with the majority. They began to join the political parties that were in the forefront of the political struggle for independence. They had cast their lot fully with the majority of the people.

On the opposite side, those at the Coast were not at ease. They felt that they would not be incorporated fully into the new body politic. They were apprehensive about the new political dispensation. They expressed the fear that their interests would not be considered. They even entertained the idea that their future could be tied with that of Zanzibar. Worried as they were, they were even playing with the idea of some sort of autonomy. They were of the opinion that they should not be part of the newly emerging independent nation of Kenya, and that they would be better off to stand alone without being part of the new nation (Chande 2000: 349).

The feeling of marginalization was rampant after independence was realized fully and the country was running its own affairs. Globalization was also having an impact in this connection. Developments in the Middle East and Iran were exerting their share of influence. Muslims were feeling an increasing affinity with the global Muslim community, the *Umma*. They were also exposed to education, both local and external. Internally, Muslims joined the institutions of higher learning and began to find their place in the wider discussion that opened up through education. Many Muslims also found themselves studying abroad, especially in the Middle East. They came with a heightened consciousness of their

Muslim identity. Many preachers were at the same time ready to express their opinion through their preaching in the mosques. Issues such as education, aspects of *Sharia*, the wearing of head scarves in schools, and other concerns came to the open and became issues for discussion now and then. In the course of time, they raised new concerns that would have an effect on the wider society.

In this connection, one episode stands out. The Muslims at the Coast began to agitate for the formation of an exclusively Islamic party, the Islamic Party of Kenya (IPK). This politico-religious step and the activities related to it became a hot issue on the national scene. Heated arguments for and against it took place. Both Muslims and Christians were exchanging accusations and counter accusations. The exchanges showed unequivocally that the situation was undergoing important changes that would cast a shadow over the future. Odde presents the various events that transpired in this connection as follows:

> Widespread feelings of discrimination among Muslims were exploited by extremists, leading to serious outbreaks of violence in 1992–1994 in Mombasa…Archbishop Manasses Kuria of the CPK strongly criticized Muslim activity against Christianity and warned that their incitement could ignite a religious war…There was a sharp reaction from Muslim leaders…In 1993, Jeff Mbure, an NCCK activist, wrote an article expressing apprehension that Kenya was becoming an arena for Muslim-Christian conflict and that Islamic fundamentalism threatened the country's future. The tension, he warned, would intensify, and that what is happening in North Africa would be a child's play compared to the conflicts in store for Kenya. (Odde 2000: 106)

The move to establish an exclusively Muslim party was opposed by the government of the day. The proponents of the idea were denied registration. The decision of the state became a source of Muslim dissatisfaction. Demonstrations were organized in opposition to the decision. This was followed by a series of riots that caused material damages and death. The issue had raised the political temperature so high that a renowned Muslim scholar, Professor Ali Mazrui, warned of serious consequences if the Muslim demand in this regard was not heeded by the government. The Muslim demand for the creation of a separate party based on religion and the reaction to such a call by both the government and the public at large also show that the disagreements were serious indeed.

Ali Mazrui's prediction of a future *Intifada* against the Kenyan government by Swahili-speaking people in Kenya's Coast Province, should the
IPK be prevented from participating in future general elections, is not to
be dismissed out of hand. It is one form of possible politico-religious conflict in the future. Nor should the position of Somali-speaking Muslims
as soldiers and petty traders be ignored as another source of potential
political strife in Kenya. (Twaddle 1995: 7)

Christians were also concerned at this stage with reference to a resolution made in January 1981. At a meeting held in Mecca, Saudi Arabia,
the Organization of Islamic Conference (OIC) had passed a resolution
calling for "*jihad* against infidels," "to liberate the territories" in which
Muslims live and to propagate Islam. This resolution generated a lot of
anger among Kenyan Christians. The call from the OIC had serious
repercussions and elicited many negative reactions from Christians in the
country. The warning signals could not be ignored.

There were also other issues that concerned the Muslim communities. Questions about alleged discrimination against Muslims regarding employment opportunities in government departments, educational
institutions, as well as equitable share of media time were being raised
with greater passion and intensity. New developments had given Muslims
the opportunity to air their views in a hitherto unfettered way.

There was a lot of political agitation in favor of opening up the political space during the second half of President Arap Moi's presidency.
There was increased political activity for the introduction of multiparty
democracy. Many politicians and civil society groups were fighting for
the creation of political parties. This period was dubbed the fight for
the "second liberation." Many up-and-coming leaders strove to change
the political scene by bringing about the end of one party rule. The
Christian churches were in the forefront of this struggle for a new democratic dispensation (Throup 1995: 143–176; Benson 1995: 177–179;
Hizkias and Wachira 1996). Many church leaders and their followers
confronted the government in support of changes. As a predominantly
Christian nation, the churches had taken upon themselves to participate
in the political forum to bring forth change. Consequently, their voices
proved very powerful and decisive in the long run. They could not be
ignored indefinitely.

At first, one could thus say that the stage of political agitation was
dominated by Christians. They remained the main actors who shaped
the political situation. Gradually, however, the scenario began to change.

Once multiparty democracy became the order of the day, the voices of the Muslim community were also being raised and taken into consideration. On the one hand, voices from this religious group found their place in the public forum. Even though they had earlier stood aside, they now saw the need to do something. They recognized the need to express their positions on issues that affected them. They began to organize themselves and to present their communal voices. On the other hand, they began to be wooed by different parties for their votes. Consequently, they became conscious of their weight in the political arena. Their votes counted and they were courted. As their significance gained ground, they began to speak for themselves and argue on the interests of their communities.

NEW VOICES

There are a number of issues that are bringing the Muslim presence into the limelight. All these issues have become strong talking points in the national forum. First, Muslims have become a force to be reckoned with and are important in the electoral process. Their numbers are contested. They oscillate between 10 and 30 percent. While the former is said to be the national estimate from government sources, Muslims argue that their numbers are as high as the latter. As parties proliferate and hunt for votes, every individual as well as a community become important players that are sought by the leadership of the numerous parties, especially during the election period. As the number of political parties grows and they jostle for important positions, there is no question that every vote counts. Previously sitting on the sidelines, Muslims have now become conscious of the influence they can exert on the political scene (Warigi 2007: 19).

Second, even though they are being courted intensely, Muslim voices are also showing a lot of discord. While some of them want to take their rightful place in the political process, they are having a hard time to agree on what role they should play and what the issues should be. They find that their place in the political debate and arena is not as clear as it seemed earlier. Rather, it is proving to be ambiguous, to say the least (O'Brien 1995: 200–219). Some of them want to highlight what they would see as strictly Islamic issues or issues that concern specifically the Muslim community. In the event, the question of to what extent to push for Islamic values in a predominantly Christian environment becomes tricky indeed. As a result, a variety of trends are visible in the community.

To begin with, some among them argue that Muslims cannot vote as a block. They should not reflect only what they see as their religious community's concerns. Rather, considering the environment in which they live, they have to participate in the electoral process only as individuals. Abdurahman Bafadhil makes a very interesting argument in this direction:

It is, therefore, logical to say that beyond the strict issues of religion—our belief in Allah and adherence to the Holy Prophet—Muslims in Kenya are different in their secular concerns…Islam cannot be used to garner political following for a human being…Every Muslim in Kenya has a right to make his or her independent decision on who to support for the presidency…There was no Western-style democracy in Islam…Islam is a theocracy…And since there is no Islamic theocracy in Kenya, a predominantly Christian country, Muslims cannot participate in politics on religious assumptions. (2007: 11)

Although this argument on the general approach to politics has not reached its logical conclusion yet, there are other issues that are engaging the Muslim community. Top on the list and one which may be said to summarize the general feeling is the one on marginalization, which has already been referred to earlier. Very strong views are being expressed in this connection. Some Muslims are of the opinion that they and their community have been marginalized even though they represent a significant number of the population. As a minority, they claim that their interests have not been addressed in comparison with the larger population. They argue that discrimination against them as Muslims has in a way become the practice of successive governments that have ruled the country. The following is a complaint that is expressed by some Muslim leaders:

Over the years, Muslims, who are the largest minority in the country, feel that they have suffered the most flagrant forms of discrimination—more than any other Kenyan community at the hands of successive governments…Many Muslims feel that the Government has victimized them in the so-called war on terror…While the constitution guarantees equal rights to all Kenyans, Muslims have lost faith in the supreme law of the land, for the last 44 years, their grievances have not been addressed, and their inalienable rights have been violated. (Ayman 2007: 11)

The issue of marginalization is a grave one indeed. Whether it is a perception by the victim or a true reflection of reality, it does not augur well for the future unless it is addressed to the satisfaction of all parties concerned. If things are to fall in line, then those who feel victimized must reach a stage where they feel that their grievances have been taken seriously when they are aired. They should also feel that there is ample room for rectification and that appropriate policies put in place and steps taken to address the concerns. As is the case in many societies wracked by violence and civil war, the feeling of exclusion, unless addressed early, could often give rise to and fuel violent reactions. Once people feel excluded from a system and do not see a way out of the exclusion, they often resort to violence. Violent reactions become the only options left for a group that feels shut out of a system that it considers unjust and unresponsive to its demands.

It is not only marginalization that Muslims are complaining about. The connection with Somalia, in terms of both ethnicity (for those who come from the north where ethnic Somalis dominate) and religion raise the stakes for the future. Professor Ali Mazrui puts it as follows:

> The radicalization of Kenyan Somalis, if we continue to marginalize them and humiliate them, is a real possibility and the radicalization of other Muslims in Kenya has to be taken into account. At least the danger is more in terms of intifada, the black intifada scenario I mentioned earlier, rather than recruitment into Al Qaeda. (Smith 2007: 44–48)

From some such statements, one may gather the idea that the situation in Somalia is close to the heart of the Muslim community in Kenya. This is not strange in the light of the history of Kenya. Going back as far as 1964, the northern part of Kenya had sometimes entertained the idea of merging with Somalia. The ethnic and religious pull of the "Somali nation" proved to be strong at times. This had led to a brief skirmish between Somalia and Kenya in 1964. Notwithstanding decisive roles played by Kenyans of Somali extraction in the history of the country, there is no question that mixed sentiments can pop up sometimes. As the civil war rages on in Somalia and it increases in intensity, some Muslims have expressed serious concerns about its development. There are also a number of other issues that are related to it.

First, there is a general concern that the war in Somalia had gotten out of hand. It has had adverse effects both on the Somali people themselves and on their ethnic counterparts who live on this side of the Kenyan border. They have expressed strong feelings that the war has to come to an end. Muslims in Kenya also seem to feel that they have to contribute something to a conflict that has dragged on for so long not only as members of the same ethnic group but also as brothers in the faith. Whatever their feelings on the conflict, they express their opinion that the Kenyan government must use its position and influence to bring it to an end. They have urged the government to act as a peace broker in view of the advantage that Kenya has in being well placed to play a leading and positive role. They have also taken it upon themselves to voice their protest in support of Muslims in Somalia whenever they feel that the latter have been treated adversely by others. Muslims have urged President Kibaki to rally African leaders in seeking a lasting solution to the mayhem in Somalia…They accused the Ethiopian army of abusing the rights of Somali Muslims by bombing and storming mosques. "Last month, the Ethiopian army stormed a mosque in Somalia and killed 21 people including 8 sheiks. Their acts are a desecration of holy places of worship. The soldiers also stormed a hospital and killed patients before looting drugs and other medical equipment" (Omanga 2008: 4). The interesting fact is that no such vehement condemnation is uttered when similar desecration of Christian or Muslim holy places is carried out in Somalia by Muslims themselves. The destruction of Christian churches and Muslim (Sufi) cemeteries in some parts of Somalia is a case in point.

Second, while calling on the Kenyan government to use its good offices to bring about lasting peace, they also see as their duty to express their grudge against Ethiopia. There are two sides to the story of the stand against Ethiopia. On the one hand, there is a strong opposition to the involvement of Ethiopian troops and their activities in Somalia. Whether based on ethnic or religious intentions, Muslims are opposed to the Ethiopian army's adventure into Somalia. One suspects here that, in addition to the bad blood that had existed between Ethiopia and Somalia, which flared up occasionally in armed confrontations in the past, Muslims believe that a Christian country has no right to invade a Muslim country. Therefore, the religious element plays a role here. On the other hand, some events and practices related to the treatment of some people of Somali or Kenyan origin allegedly related to the insurgency in Somalia has also become a hot issue. Some of the people who were captured in the course of the fighting in Somalia have been sent to Ethiopia. What has been called "extraordinary rendition" has thus become an emotional issue. Muslims raise objections to the practice of handing over these people to Ethiopia. Their incarceration in Ethiopian jails, their treatment and the general idea of sending them to another country instead of bringing them to justice in Kenya, have become burning issues. Further still, the question of the involvement of Kenyan Somalis in the war in Somalia is a hot issue. This concerns recruitment of young people to fight in the war, financial assistance to the warring parties, especially to the radical groups, and so on.

Third, this is closely related to the issue of terrorism. Some Muslim leaders express the opinion that what they see as the "unholy alliance" between Ethiopia and the United States in pursuing what they called terrorists is misplaced. In fact, they argue that it targets the Muslim community unfairly. Furthermore, it casts aspersion on Islam by portraying Islam as a religion that supports terrorism. This, it is argued by Muslims, is a position perpetrated by enemies of Islam and distorts the truth about their religion. The questions persist and are posed intermittently as they provoke the ire of the Muslim community. Question: "Some people have been associating Islam with terrorism?" Answer: "That is a scheme of the western world and Israel against Muslims and Islam...The Quran is revelations of God's word, tradition and prophets and saying of prophets. The two have no place for extremism. Extremism [sic] are imaginations of people who want to portray Islam negatively" (Wachu 2008: 16).

In this issue of terrorism as well as other complaints of marginalization, the Muslim community expresses its opinion that it is viewed in a negative light. It is made to carry responsibility for acts that it has nothing to do with. It is persecuted for events that in no way are connected with the community or the religion. However strong and insistent the disclaimers might be, the complaints and accusations pile up and raise the temperature to a higher degree.

All these issues seem to form an explosive mix that point to an uncertain future. In the face of such challenges, however, there are also reassuring voices in this regard. The words of Adan Wachu, the secretary-general of the Supreme Council of Kenya Muslims (SUPKEM), are reassuring indeed: "This nation has not experienced religious confrontation. I don't see that happening. We will continue to live in this nation as brothers and sisters." (Wachu 2008: 16) Comforting words indeed in situations that otherwise invoke all kinds of grievances. The center is holding well for the moment in the face of all these complaints. Only time will tell for how long such noble sentiments will be able to hold together all the tensions that are pulling in different directions.

TANZANIA

By all accounts, Tanzania has been viewed as the model of coexistence when it comes to ethnic and religious diversity in Africa. Under the leadership of its veteran President Mwalimu Julius Nyerere, it had successfully forged the image of a nation where all sorts of differences could be accommodated. In this sense, it has been seen as a shining example for numerous African countries beset by civil conflicts inspired by religion and ethnicity. There are increasing concerns about how long such an ideal situation might last. Numerous incidents point to the fact that the peace for which Tanzania has been rightly known and commended for may be wobbling. Religion is becoming the main issue in this changing social and political environment. This trend is acknowledged by no less than the current president of the country, Jackaya Kikwete, himself:

> During Kenya's 2005 referendum on the draft constitution and the December 2007 General Election, religious hate material was traded, with Christians and Muslims expressing fears of potential domination by the other...President Kikwete observed that religious utterances were a potential threat to Africa's fragile democracies. Kikwete, a Muslim, who has repulsed attempts to "Islamise" his Government, said "while political chaos (in Kenya) was inspired by ethnic hatred, political divisions in Tanzania were determined by religious affiliations. This is not to suggest that a similar thing (political chaos) cannot occur here. Tribalism is almost alien in Tanzania, although we are multi-ethnic. However, Tanzania has *udini* (religionism), which is not as pronounced in Kenyan politics," he said. (Mpinganjira 2008: 27)

If one takes this quotation as a point of departure, one notes that there are numerous challenges regarding religious coexistence in Tanzania. In the first place, there is concern expressed from various sides that one religious group might dominate the other. In a situation where the number of adherents of both religions is equally divided, as is the case with Tanzania, the contest becomes more pronounced. It helps sometimes when there are more than two actors on the ethnic and religious scene, which is not the case here. Second, in the case of Tanzania, the issue of religion has taken the upper hand over the questions of race or ethnic origin. In the political scene, the issue of religion has gained in importance. Religion is becoming a force to be reckoned with in the ordering of the social and political life of the nation.

As we saw was the case with Kenya, the Muslim voice in Tanzania is becoming more vocal than hitherto. Again, just like Kenya, the Muslims in Tanzania are complaining more and more about being marginalized. They argue that their participation on the national and governmental levels is limited. In their view, it is not commensurate with their numbers. Again, in their view, the government of Tanzania is run mostly by Christians. As a result, they claim that it is lopsided when it comes to attending to their needs and rights. In such an atmosphere, seizing power even through the ballot box becomes a serious contest. Election periods become contests when the adherents of the two religions fight over the way to seize the reins of power.

Other than elections, the mistrust between Muslims and Christians seems to have grown since 1985 when the first Muslim President, Hassan Mwinyi, was elected. Ever since, a number of events added fuel to a feeling of unease, to say the least. Suddenly, violence erupted where some Christian institutions were burned and young children killed in the process. In 1993, Muslims also rioted in the commercial capital of the country, Dar-es-Salaam. The bone of contention at this time was the sale of pork, considered as unholy food. Some Muslims who objected to such a sale took matters into their own hands and burned shops that were selling pork. Furthermore, the language of Muslim preachers was becoming more strident and provocative. As the tensions grew, there were instances when Christian literature and Bibles were burned. Mock public debates conducted by Muslims and video cassettes brought mainly from outside the country targeting the Christian faith adversely began to surface.

Rumors also played their part. One of them was that Zanzibar, the island predominantly inhabited by Muslims, had secretly joined the OIC. This generated a lot of discussion among the people. Many Christians were worried that these were preliminary steps to make Tanzania an Islamic country. Muslim countries were also increasing the tension by opening embassies in Zanzibar.

The marginalization that Muslims claim is their lot in Tanzania is more pronounced in the area of education and political power, in their view. In the former, they argue that educational establishments were heavily stacked against Muslims. Christians were much more favored in the educational sector. The Nyerere government often saw these complaints as a threat to Tanzanian political and social stability. In some instances, the advocates of such demands were isolated and even detained (Chande 2000: 360). Muslims had also complained that *Sharia* courts have not been instituted in line with what they see as their wishes and rights. Some Tanzanian Muslims even argue that since they are the majority of the population in the country, they have to have a bigger say on the way the country is run. Consequently, in their opinion, Tanzania should be declared a Muslim country. Some extremist preachers deliberately front the argument that they cannot be ruled by "*kaffirs*" (unbelievers) and that Muslims have to be prepared for a *Jihad*. Such developments are viewed with trepidation by Christians. They fear that once this is the case, they would be second-class citizens in their own country. The suspicions thus pile up to the detriment of the social fabric.

Another boiling area is Zanzibar. This is becoming a thorn in the flesh of the government of Tanzania. Zanzibar and Tanganyika were wedded into a union in 1964. Zanzibar is predominantly Muslim. In recent years, there has been an increased consciousness of Muslim identity in the island. On the basis of its emphasis on Muslim perspectives and world-view, the island has been looking more to the Middle East for guidance and leadership in matters of governance and religion. Young people were sent to these countries to study and their views on Islam intensified.

> Islamic assertiveness in Tanzania has been more evident in Zanzibar. Young people have increasingly and openly identified with an Islamic trend in this mainly Muslim society that has special status in the Tanzanian union. The Tanzanian government has worried about the upsurge in Islamic activism on the island. (Kwayera 2008: 36)

From the Christian perspective, there are many internal and external activities that are spearheading and spreading the Muslim cause. Local organizations are joining international Muslim organizations such as Islam in Africa Project. There are also calls for Tanzania to join the OIC. Agitations by Muslim preachers and even invitations to riots are encouraged by some radical elements in their ranks. Elected Muslim officials are also prodded to promote Islamic concerns such as *Sharia* and the institution of Muslim jurisprudence. Public servants and government officials are expected by their Muslim constituencies to favor Muslims and promote their welfare.

The overall result is that the country is going backward with regard to its harmonious past. Racial and religious schools that were few in the past are now becoming almost normal. Worse still, the atmosphere is becoming tense and foreboding. The conclusions of a book on this changing environment are not comforting indeed:

> While its 10 ethnic groups have lived without serious friction since independence, religion is proving to be quite another matter. Over the last fifteen years, it has been apparent that religion has the potential of becoming a social tinderbox…If what is happening in Rwanda and Burundi is anything to go by, it is clear the price for real or imagined injustices can be high. In the twin Central African countries, thousands have perished because a group of people feel they have been denied justice and have been transformed into minions in their own country. Muslims in Tanzania are registering frightfully similar sentiments today. (Wijsen and Mfumbusa 2004: 15, 75)

From what has been said earlier regarding Kenya and Tanzania, one can discern that there are a number of factors that increase the temperature in connection with religion and violence. First, there is a marked feeling of marginalization by the Muslim communities. They believe that they have been discriminated against especially when it concerns positions in government offices and education. This feeling has been based on the experiences and practices related to the colonial era: Since Muslims tended to avoid going to mission schools or were excluded from them, Christians came to have a 'privileged position' in society. With the rise of literate Africans, Muslims became less important to the colonial administration, and Muslim communities tended to become marginalized from the modern economic sector. The imbalances created by these unequal colonial circumstances make up much of the legacy being experienced by the Muslim peoples of East Africa to this day (Sperling and Kagabo 2000: 297).

Second, and worse still, they claim that their grievances have not been addressed adequately when aired. Even when they made representations, the mistakes have not been rectified in their view. Some state and public reactions also show that the respective governments did not know how to deal with the demands that were raised by the Muslims. Sometimes, there was an attempt to sideline the spokespeople or to ban them altogether or to isolate them. In other cases, the agitators were persecuted and punished. Some governments also tried their hands in playing the game of divide and rule. They sowed discord among the actors and let them fight against each other.

Third, even in the face of such confusion, there is no question that the Muslim voice has become increasingly shrill. They have taken the advantage of the democratic space to express their views, which sometimes become provocative. Even so, the voices have also been discordant. As the case in Kenya shows, there is no clear direction as to how to participate in the political arena. Although some have opted to throw themselves into the political game as full citizens, others shy away by elevating the Muslim agenda. Considering these factors, the way to deal with the Muslim communities becomes increasingly a challenge for both Muslims and Christians. The problem of finding an optimum political space where Christians and Muslims can participate fully becomes paramount.

This delicate situation in itself is complicated even further by other factors that have an external dimension. First, the global Islamic "resurgence or revival," however one wants to refer to it, has certainly an impact on the local level. Increased cooperation and interaction with the wider Muslim world has become a source of strength, education, and inspiration for Muslims. Many ideas that are operating on the global stage are finding local reception and expression. Not only ideas but also finances from these sources strengthen local activities. Such influences have two effects: on the one hand, they pit the locals against one another. Although some are fully receptive and bent on propagating the new ideas, others resist. At some point, the confrontations may turn violent. This will eventually invite the attention of the authorities who have to react. Second, the authorities find themselves in a difficult situation when their legitimacy is questioned. Some of these movements are aggressively pushing for an Islamic political and social regime. The militants among them want to force their way into the society. As we saw in some instances, violence is even practiced to make a point in this direction. Third, the wind of war and violence blowing from Somalia cannot be wholly avoided. It has affected the region one way or another. Events in Somalia as well as in Kenya show that debates rage on events that take place in Somalia or in connection with it. The question of "rendition" is a case in point. The question of the respective government's participation in the conflict in Somalia is another. How should governments in this region respond to events in Somalia? Should they, being predominantly Christian, venture into that soil, which is Muslim? How does one deal with Muslim sensitivities on this matter? Fourth, and more ominous, the bombings in August 1998 have elicited fears, suspicions, and debates on many sides.

The question of "terrorism" and its relationship with Islam and Muslims is being asked with greater intensity. On the one hand, the wider society is prone to point an accusing finger on Muslims and Islam. On the other hand, Muslims complain about being unfairly targeted for acts that neither themselves as believers nor their faith condones. The least that can be said is that suspicions will continue to mount if present trends persist. Such an atmosphere of mistrust does not augur well for the peaceful resolution of the problem of marginalization felt by Muslims in these countries. As we saw in the case of Tanzania, the prospect of violent conflict thus hangs in the air.

One ray hope in these developments is the way religious leaders come together and deliberate on public issues of common concern. These leaders who belong to various faiths sit together from time to time and sift through the political happenings in the country to reach a consensus on their assessment of the state of the countries. The direction of the governments, the state of the nation, the conduct of government, to name a few, do draw them together. In their own inimitable way, they comment on all issues that touch and affect the life of the nations. They sit down together, thrash out the issues, stand together and issue statements that contribute to healthy discussions. Such common moves are very significant in such otherwise volatile situations. There is no doubt that such contributions from religious leaders will exert a positive influence on interreligious coexistence.

The foregoing has shown how Christian-Muslim relations may be a source of conflict in Kenya and Tanzania. On its part, Uganda also shares with them some characteristics that we will look at. At the same time, Uganda offers us a glimpse into another form of violence. On the one hand, this has to do entirely with a Christian-inspired movement. It claims to be based on the vision of establishing a faith-based political regime. On the other hand, it also claims to represent the grievances of northern Uganda against its government. Whatever the case, the violence unleashed in 1986 has unfortunately spawned many years and inflicted immense brutality on its victims. Let us now turn to Uganda.

UGANDA

To begin with, one notes that Uganda has also been the playground of two religions. In terms of history, Islam arrived in Uganda in 1860 from the Eastern coast ahead of Christianity. It had also moved with some people in connection with their sojourn from the Sudan. This was the first period when Muslims shone and had prominence over their Christian counterparts. There was no other religion on the scene that could rival them when they arrived in the country in the nineteenth century. In the event, Islam was almost close to becoming the state religion. Anglican Christians arrived only in 1877. For some time after, there was good cooperation among Christians and Muslims. They even collaborated in overthrowing king (Kabaka) Mwanga of Buganda in 1888. At first, he was good at playing the two faiths against each other. He was outwitted later. In 1892, the two wings of Christianity, Anglicans and Catholics, declared war on each other. Their division was short-lived. They brought their forces together when another war broke out in 1898. The defeat of the Muslims proved decisive in relegating them to the periphery of Ugandan political life for years to come until the arrival of Idi Amin in 1971.

With the arrival of the British in Uganda, Islam faced a formidable foe. In contrast to their policies toward the Muslim faith in some of their colonies, for instance, Nigeria, the British did not look favorably at Islam in Uganda. Rather, they tried their best to limit its influence. For whatever reasons, they did not see that their interests were served by the spread of Islam. Therefore, they encouraged Christianity to take root in the country and opened it up to Christianity's predominance. The second time when Muslims had shone was when Idi Amin took over the reins of power and became the president of Uganda in 1971. With his ascension to power, Muslims found favor in many ways; they also reaped some benefits. When thousands of Asians were expelled in 1972, for example, they benefited a lot in economic terms. They took most of the property that belonged to the expellees. They were also allowed to practice their faith in celebrating their holidays. These ups and downs in the fortunes of Muslims also define the relationships they had with their Christian counterparts. As one writer puts it, "Uganda's political history is a tale of competition between Islam and Christianity and between Roman Catholic and Protestants—struggles that are charged by numerous issues, historical, political and socio-economic" (Chande 2000: 354).

One of the interesting aspects of the overall situation that prevailed in Uganda is the persistence of violence. Once referred to as the "pearl of Africa" by the one time British Prime Minister Winston Churchill it was often bogged down in violence In the early years of independence, the country brimmed with optimism just as many other sub-Saharan African countries. Many factors were working for the country. To begin with, the first Prime Minister, Milton Obote, had promised to bring all the ethnic groups together under one nation. He was even willing to serve as the head of government under "the Kabaka," the king of Buganda—a monarchy in Uganda. In this arrangement, Sir Edward Mutesa, the king, would serve as the head of state.

Gradually, however, Obote felt too constricted by the prevailing political arrangement. He deemed it necessary to concentrate power in his hands. To this end, he used the police force to harass and imprison some of the members of his cabinet who did not toe the line. To further consolidate power in his hands, he planned to oust the king and assume the presidency. When the parliament of the Buganda kingdom tried to challenge him, he ordered his army commander Idi Amin to arrest the king. Going beyond his orders, Amin stormed the residence of the king and forced him into exile. Many of the followers and sympathizers of the king were later imprisoned or forced into exile themselves. Obote abolished the monarchy and installed a one-party state. From then on, he used his special security apparatus to hunt his opponents under a series of states of emergency. The seeds of violence that would haunt Uganda for years to come have been sown by the first president. It was not long before he himself was stripped of his power by his closest ally, Idi Amin, and forced into exile until the next time.

In 1971, Idi Amin toppled Obote and took over power. Some, especially the Baganda (the people of the kingdom of Buganda), welcomed the change, even hailing Amin as a savior. The euphoria was short-lived. Amin turned Uganda into a living hell. Under him, everything collapsed; the country was thrown into anarchy. Thousands were killed. Many also left for exile. Anyone in leadership who challenged him was eliminated. Ugandans had to endure years of brutality under Idi Amin. It was only the intervention of the Tanzanian army and Ugandan guerillas in 1979 that managed to bring the Amin regime to an end. Even the change went awry from the start. The incoming foreign troops who were received as liberators looted what was left in the country. The citizens also took part in the rampage in what was viewed as revenge against Amin. Finally, the return of Obote to power through the support of President Nyerere of Tanzania only succeeded in exacerbating the situation. Rebel movements sprouted and created havoc in the country. The five-year civil war proved extremely devastating to the people. It was only after the

National Resistance Movement (NRM), one of the rebel groups led by current President Yoweri Museveni, took power in 1986 that a semblance of order began to take shape. Even then, as we shall see in the section on the LRA, the whole country did not enjoy the peace dividend.

Many have posed the question as to why violence persisted in Uganda throughout its history beginning from independence. In fact, some have presented the notion of peace in Uganda as a strange phenomenon. In the light of the violent history, a situation where peace reigned would be something the people is unaccustomed to. In this view, it would be difficult to handle peace (Buwembo 2008: 14).

It is now believed that religion had had a hand in the violence. It played a significant role in the political history of Uganda. Early on, the membership and leadership of the dominant political parties were drawn from the two main Christian groups. While the Catholics were organized under the banner of the Democratic Party (DP), the Protestants did so under the Uganda People's Congress (UPC). One of the merits of the Protestants was that they courted the Muslims who obliged. Unfortunately for the latter, they were beset by internal dissensions that made a common front impossible. Consequently, the dominant political forces used the dissension to their advantage by worsening the cleavages. The churches supported different leaders and played one Muslim leader against another.

On the whole, religion tied to ethnicity played a detrimental role in the Ugandan scene. The main culprits were the two Christian churches and their various ethnic bases. The conflict was both within and without. Internally, the members were often involved in squabbles on issues of power. They coupled this with ethnic interests that often defined their constituencies. Their desire was to establish "ethnically homogenous dioceses." On the external or national level, the two prominent churches often contradicted each other. They fought each other to maintain power in one way or another especially by getting closer to the government of the day. The two political parties were used as fronts for the church members who served as their leaders. Conflicts were fuelled as a result of the competition between them and the contradictions that obtained among them. They could not find any common ground on the basis of a national agenda that tied them together.

This does not mean at all that there were no leaders who tried to offer alternative leadership that served the people justly, like Bishop Festus Kivengere. They were often attacked by the government of the day or weakened by the splits that operated in the churches. This was exacerbated by the fact that, in some cases, the political positions of the parties were even confounded with that of the divine. Voting for one party was sometimes viewed as a religious obligation supported by a religious truth. In the end, their antagonisms based on their religious convictions fuelled violent conflicts that proved catastrophic for the country. One conclusion is unequivocal about the role of the churches in the violent conflicts (Ward 1995: 98; for an opposite view, see Waliggo 1995: 118).

Regarding the fate of the Muslim community, a better opportunity seemed to have come to them with the seizure of power by Idi Amin who was a Muslim. He brought to an end the constant wrangling that had earlier beset them. He united them under one leadership and organization. He also helped them to establish institutions to deal with specific Muslim concerns. He further strengthened the Muslims by extending their connection with countries in the Middle East. He was instrumental and keen in establishing relationships with Muslim countries such as Saudi Arabia, Libya, and Iran (Kokole 1995: 45–55). In this connection, many Muslims were provided the opportunity to go for further training in these countries. The relationship also came with considerable financial assistance. This in turn helped to open educational establishments that catered exclusively to the Muslim community. Even though Muslims numbered 10–15 percent of the population, such educational institutions were lacking up to this moment. The coming of Idi Amin was thus a big boost to the community. In fact, the most decisive step that had long-term implications in this regard was that Uganda became a member of the OIC. It was a decision that could not be overturned even after thirty years of regime change (Kasozi 1995: 237).

Educational opportunities offered to Muslims gave them an opening to the outside world, especially, the Islamic world. As a result, there were palpable changes in the activities of Muslims. There were also changes in the rhetoric and the contents of the sermons delivered by those who returned from abroad. There was a new tone of militancy and reaching out to the greater Muslim community. A new awareness was growing with its own demands.

There were growing disagreements within the Muslim ranks on issues that touched Muslim identity and sense of direction. After the fall of Idi Amin and especially in the 1990s, the disagreements were fuelled by a radical element that was injected into the community. One of the new developments had to do with the relationship of the community to the civil courts. In the course of tensions that arose as a result of disagreements, the issue had to be taken to the Supreme Court that decided on the case. This move was rejected by one party in the dispute that declared the civil court as "an infidel (*kaffir*) court." Such a position was followed by riots in which several people were killed. A new face of radical Islam that questioned the civil institutions had emerged. A new challenge was being presented to the wider society. Some were openly advocating that *Sharia* become the guiding principle in the life of Muslims. In the same line, some were calling for the defiance of civil authority. The question of whether Muslims need to subject themselves to a secular court became crucial.

In the long run, such a tendency would somehow cast a shadow on the way societies are administered. The road to reach a social contract and consensus would be tested severely. By proposing a new dimension as to how a society is run, some members of the Muslim community were throwing down the gauntlet to the wider society. The line between expressing a difference of opinion on a vital issue and resorting to violence to impose one's will was becoming too thin:

> Around the same time, the Uganda Muslim Liberation Army (UMLA) was formed to champion the rights of Muslims against what they saw as the Museveni government's disregard for their rights and interests. They accused the Museveni government of attempting to undermine their religion and their community by converting mosques into offices as part of a policy to return several properties formerly under the control of UMSC (the Uganda Muslim Supreme Council, created by Amin in an effort to bring together the various Muslim factions who were fighting for the leadership of the Muslim community) to their former Asian owners. Socioeconomic forces were clearly at play here: when Muslims, as a minority, call for the establishment of an Islamic government to replace the "kaffir" one, they are speaking the rights and privileges of "full citizenship" that they feel they have been denied. (Chande 2000: 355)

As we had discussed earlier, the history of Uganda has been turbulent since independence. There have been cases of violent conflicts throughout a greater part of its history (Kasozi 1994). For reasons that have been mentioned briefly above, some of the violent conflicts that rocked the country had had a religious cover. A more sinister group soon invaded the landscape and tried to impose its religious vision. It took up arms to impose this religious solution on the government of the day and the population that was found in its area of operation. This group that unleashed one of the long-lasting and devastating religion-inspired movements was of a semi-Christian origin. It concerns the infamous Lord's Resistance Army (LRA). It is now time to turn to deal with it in some detail.

LRA

Times of crises often give birth to strange human responses and activities. The period between the fall of Idi Amin and that of Obote, 1979–1986, was a time of great and rampant violence in Uganda. Many rebel movements roamed the land. All nursed various grievances and mushroomed in a chaotic environment. All of them had a lot to do with violence. By all accounts, Uganda was immersed in a devastating civil war. It was in this period that one of the movements that persisted for many years to come had its origins. It was inspired by religious motivations and was later called the LRA. Before it assumed its final shape and this particular name, it was preceded by two leaders (Behrend 1995: 59–67). In the first place, there was a father, Saverino Lukoya, who claimed to have had a special vision about what was to happen in the future. After suffering a fall and being unconscious for some time, he felt that he was transported to heaven. He then dreamt that one of his children would be subject to visitation by many spirits. It followed that one of his daughters, Alice Auma, was the woman who would receive the spirits and found a movement.

In 1985, she felt possessed by a spirit. On the basis of her account, the spirit was sent by God to northern Uganda. She believed that she had received a special inspiration to launch an armed movement. One of her main goals was to overthrow the government in place at that time. Her mission was spiritual. "She was possessed by a spirit called Lakwena, who ordered her to build up the HSMF (Holy Spirit Mobile Forces), in order to bring down the government, purify the world of sin, and build up a new world in which humans and nature would be reconciled" (Behrend 1998: 109). It was an all encompassing mission that included many facets. Its kernel was the creation of a new dispensation built on the cleansing of the old from its ills and the building of a new one in its place.

In her mission to purify the world and to create a new one that will be in harmony with nature, Alice had instruments of war at her disposal. She believed that she was possessed with spiritual powers and that bullets would hurt neither herself nor her fellow combatants, reminiscent of what was the case among the combatants in Liberia. To this end, she practiced many rituals that had to do with nature. For instance, whenever her followers crossed a river, they had to make an offering to get the permission and consent of the spirits of the water. If the offering and the rituals are not deemed correct or acceptable, the spirits may refuse to grant the passage requested. The decision by the water spirits has to be respected. Wild animals of the forest, such as snakes among others, were also viewed as supporters and collaborators of these holy warriors. On the whole, nature was believed to be on the side of the soldiers, and it demanded respect in return. Nature could fight on their behalf and on their side if it was given its due; it could attack their enemies. If not respected, it would also turn against them.

Many followed Alice Lakwena after they saw that she had succeeded in routing the government forces at least in the beginning. Later, however, she proved no match for the better organized forces of the Ugandan government and their weapons. As a result, she was forced to abandon her efforts. She left for exile and lived in a refugee camp in Kenya and died there eventually. Her father tried to pick up where she left but was eventually unsuccessful. After being captured and imprisoned, he was released and founded a church in the north of the country.

The unsuccessful efforts of Alice Lakwena and her father would be continued by a more sinister organization that benefited from their defeat. The former rival who was ridiculed by Alice Lakwena when he proposed a joint assault on Kampala would become a formidable successor. Her cousin Joseph Kony became her heir. He adopted many of the spiritual concepts and rituals that were part and parcel of the practices of Alice Lakwena. In his own way, "Kony claims to be sent by God to make people follow God and lead them to a new world. His is a cleansing movement aimed at eradicating witchcraft and unbelief, and this is partly done on a Biblical basis through the powers of the Holy Spirit, partly by potent new spirits working through Kony" (Kastfelt 2005:13).

There is a very ironic and tragic twist to the movement continued by Kony. His initial aim was defined in spiritual terms. He was intent on creating a regime where the rules were based on otherworldly values. Kony was intent on establishing a theocracy that would be guided by the laws of God. In the end, however, the people for whom he supposedly fought were the victims of his project. "Joseph Kony... his ideology, he declared, was to overthrow the government and establish one that would rule according to the Bible's Ten Commandments...Kony failed to articulate any meaningful ideology...Because they were fighting within their own community, the victims of the war were their own people—the Acholi—and the LRA could not claim to represent the interests of the people it was killing" (Kalinaki 2006: i).

The end result turned out to be completely opposite to the original plan. Kony's experiment in the creation of divinely inspired kingdom turned awry. It created a great deal of havoc. The war that he waged led to the displacement of many people especially in the north where he came from; many lives were shattered. He also resorted to macabre tactics to bolster his war efforts. The fighters who swelled the ranks of his guerilla war were not volunteers in the majority of cases. Rather, they were mostly children and young people who were forcibly and involuntarily abducted and conscripted. The LRA was adept at attacking villages at random. It abducted children and young people. Their parents were tortured and mutilated. In some cases, the children were ordered to kill their parents so that they become hardened enough to wage atrocious battles against all kinds of enemies. Girls became sex slaves. They served as servants as well as mothers to unwanted children and future fighters.

Kony's war proved devastating. As many as 1.9 million people were uprooted from their villages and confined to what had been called "enforced encampment." The idea was to protect them from the onslaught of the rebels. It turned out that the people in the camps became hostages to their hostile environment. Uprooted from their villages and unable to live normal life, they depended on handouts from the government and aid agencies. They could neither till nor harvest and take care of themselves. They became victims of atrocities on a massive scale. Women and children became extremely vulnerable as they became targets of wanton abductions and killings. The result has been devastating:

> For 20 years, the Lord's Resistance Army—one of Africa's most feared rebel groups—has waged a vicious war in Uganda, killing civilians, mutilating people and abducting thousands of children to swell their ranks...In July, a Reuter's poll of humanitarian experts listed the 10 worst places in the world in which to be a child. Northern Uganda came second, after Sudan's war-ravaged Darfur region. The Report said 935,000 children in Northern Uganda are living in refugee camps. Some 25,000 have been abducted by the LRA since the rebellion began, it said.[1]

Northern Uganda became unlivable. It was haunted by the specter of the LRA. The situation was especially hard on the young people. Hundreds of them would be forced to leave their villages every night and seek shelters elsewhere. They tried in this way to avoid falling into the hands of the LRA. The lucky ones found shelter in the homes of relatives and friends. The rest would be forced to spend the night anywhere. In the process, they were also subjected to all kinds of harassment and even rape.

The activities of the LRA were not confined to northern Uganda. It was also a menace to the neighboring countries. Southern Sudan, the Democratic Republic of Congo, Central African Republic in their turn became victims of the atrocities committed by the LRA. Its notorious fighters roamed freely in these countries and moved from one place to the other creating havoc wherever they went. Even in these places, people were killed and children were abducted.

Many peace initiatives had been started with the aim of ending the war. Many of them failed. The signing of the peace agreement in the Sudan between the government and the SPLM/A in January 2005 opened up the possibility of bringing to an end the twenty-year-old rebellion. Peace negotiations were started between the government of Uganda and the rebel group. Important agreements were reached that raised the hope that the war was now nearing its end. Representatives of the LRA had special meetings with those of the Ugandan government. They visited the capital and met government officials. They also had meetings with their people in the north. Even so, the leader of the LRA has proved elusive so far. There were moments when everything was ready and when he was expected to sign a peace deal. All preparations were made to make this possible. He had even been given assurances and gifts (Onyango-Obbo 2007: 12). At the last minute, however, Kony simply refuses to turn up.

The end result has been that, so far, the war continues. The rebel movement has escaped all attempts to crush it militarily or bring it to the negotiating table. If this stalemate continues, the future looks bleak. During the war in Sudan, the LRA had benefited a lot due to the help it was getting from other fighting forces, including governments. If the peace agreement between the south and the north collapses for any given reason, the LRA will have a new lease on life. It will find a fertile ground for its activities if the hostilities are reignited among the belligerents in Sudan. There is no question that it will be a player in the tension that may engulf many of the countries in the region.

The LRA provides another clear example of how religion can be a source of violent conflicts. The launchers of the faith-based project looked innocent enough in the beginning. They were convinced that, with their religious faith in hand, they would create a society that would be based on religious principles. It would purify what they saw as sinful life. Never were the guidelines specified in detail at any time during the long war. But the outlines were there for all to see. The basic idea was that religion was the inspiration behind the revolt and the consequent war. Unfortunately, the holy warrior became rapacious, atrocious, and brutal. He destroyed people's lives on a massive scale. The most tragic thing is that, once the holy warrior set out on his divine mission, there was no one to convince him otherwise. There was no public arena to which he was subjected and critiqued. And the war and the mayhem continue!

CHAPTER 5

POLARIZATION OF RELIGIOUS-POLITICAL GROUPS IN THE HORN OF AFRICA

THERE ARE A NUMBER OF FAMILIAR THEMES THAT ARE PART AND PARCEL of the history of the Horn of Africa region that provide an apt commentary from the past on the present. Even though they seem to have happened a long time ago, they provide us with lessons that are pertinent even today. They characterize the relationship that exists among the two dominant religions of Christianity and Islam. In a sense, they are fixtures in the landscape and affect the lives of the region's peoples throughout their history. On the one hand, there are instances of coexistence, accommodation, and dialogue among the communities. They interact with one another and live peacefully together. There are many facets of exchange and crossing over. On the other hand, there are also instances where violent clashes predominate. In these situations, the differences that separate the religions become so acute that the only course of action becomes a violent confrontation between the communities. As a continuation of such confrontations, there are also instances where one or the other community is confined to its headquarters, marginalized, and restricted in its activities.

These happenings also give us a glimpse into the workings not only of intracommunity but also of intercommunity relationships. We observe that there were contradictions within the communities regarding how they are to relate to those outside their religious community. Some chose the way of confrontation in the attempt to preserve their identity. Others still opted to find ways of living together. In all this, some were viewed as traitors and collaborators with a community that was perceived as an enemy of the faith. Others were seen as heroes and nationalists because of their opposition to all kinds of "outsiders." The interesting thing is that, even today, these divisions and contradictory outlooks are still operating both within and without the communities of faith. The various trends and points of view have their past and present adherents. The choices of the past do not belong to the dead past. Rather, they are still seen as precursors of "correct" positions and are emulated as such or despised depending upon the point of view adopted by their followers and admirers.

PIONEER ENCOUNTER

The earliest encounter between the faiths in this region tells of an idyllic situation (Kokole 1993: 205, 233; Hiskett 1994: 137). The followers of the new religion—in this case Islam—were persecuted in their own land in Arabia. Their compatriots had rejected the new faith. The only choice open to the new believers was to leave and find refuge elsewhere. The strange and interesting fact is that they chose to cross the sea and go to a Christian country. They did this not by chance but by choice. They did not go somewhere else but agreed to move to a land where the faith was to become a competitor in the future. In fact, legend has it that it was the Prophet Muhammad himself who urged his followers to go to the host country.

On their side, the hosts proved generous. They welcomed the newcomers with open arms and offered them the refuge they sought. Indeed, at least according to prevailing legend, they went further. The two communities, the guests and the hosts, engaged in a serious but friendly dialogue on the contents of their respective faiths. The new believers were welcomed not only by the population but by the king as well. They even had a place in the palace. The king himself accorded them a peaceful environment within which they could live and practice their faith. The story also says that the king himself discussed with them his faith. The guests even went so far as to get married and find their place in the society. As Trimingham puts it, "in the fifth year of his call (A.D. 615) refugees began to cross the straits in small groups. This is referred to by Muslim writers as the first *hijra* (emigration). Later, when Muhammad had exchanged his religious mission for a political career, he arranged for those exiles who wished to return to Arabia. Some of them, however, had become Christians and where therefore the first converts from Islam to Christianity" (Trimingham 1965: 45).

As the numbers of the newcomers increased and they became self-conscious, the differences between the adherents of the two faiths began to grow. The identities of the two communities came to be defined in sharper tones. In the course of time, coexistence could not be taken for granted anymore. The two communities began to vie for supremacy. Different areas of the region came to be associated with one or the other community. In the areas where one community dominated, it fought to maintain the upper hand. It also wanted to extend its sphere of influence at the expense of the other community. Under such circumstances, war and violent confrontations became common. The consequences on many occasions proved to be devastating.

STRONG IDENTITIES

The dominant theme regarding the religious configuration of this region is that there was a core polity that saw itself as the Christian state and kingdom. Its geographic reach and its physical borders varied considerably from time to time. Even so, it always maintained that it was an entity apart. Its identity was based on the Christian faith; its core revolved around the Orthodox Church that developed its theology around the concept of a kingdom that was holy and special in the eyes of God. In fact, its teaching and history claimed that its followers constituted "the true Israel, the chosen people of God." The proof of this "spiritual and national identity" (Rubenson 1976: 408–409) was the possession of the true and original Arc of the Covenant. Just as it had defined the identity of the Jews earlier, the Arc was now central in the definition of a new identity. This followed the stealing of the Arc and taking it to Ethiopia thanks to the machinations of its king. Imbued by such a conviction, the state saw its mission as the preservation of this uniqueness against all perceived enemies. In this manner, the ties between the sacred Jewish line and the Ethiopian dynasty were intertwined unequivocally:

> The queen (Makeda) bore a son (from her union with Solomon, the king of Israel, whom she was visiting in Jerusalem), Menelik I, who traveled to Jerusalem when he came of age ... Menelik's retinue could not contemplate

life without the Ark of the Covenant, which they stole. The larceny was apparently approved by God, who levitated the youth and their holy cargo across the Red Sea before discovery and chase by Solomon's forces. The Kebra Negest's (the glory of the kings, a pastiche of legends conflated early in the fourteenth century by six Tirgrayan scribes) messages are clear: Menelik has bested his father, in a way avenging Makeda's humiliation, and God had consigned his covenant with man to Ethiopia, making it Israel's successor...The epic sought to arouse patriotic feelings of uniqueness, to glorify Ethiopia, and to provide a proud identity...Crown and church were thus inextricably linked. (Marcus 2002: 17–19)

In the past, the exclusive view was often entertained that this region was dominated by Ethiopia, "an island of Christianity" (Kapteijns 2000: 227). The prevailing view was that Muslims were marginal in this region. Recent studies have shown that Muslims were also an integral part of the picture. Even though they started late and their numbers were small in the beginning, they grew exponentially over the years. As they expanded in different directions and their strength grew, they became firmly part of the scene. They also posed as serious counterparts and challengers. In their own way, they were also equipped with a strong sense of identity that put them as a people apart. They believed that they were also a special people with a unique calling in the world. As Samatar puts it,

Muslims...shared the Islamic view. This view includes the assumption that Muslim societies belong to a universal, divinely instituted community (the so-called *umma*). Muslims therefore do not regard it as an exalted or exaggerated claim to assert that they have been assured in the Qura'n: "You have become the best community ever raised for mankind." (Sura III:110) Best be it remembered, not by ethnic distinction or racial superiority but by faith in God and by good works to the cosmic task of God's on-going plan to redeem humanity. Among the various implications of the Qura'nic prophecy, which serious Muslims must (and do) take seriously, is the universal Muslim assumption of a "historic covenant" between God and the *umma*. (1992: 4, 5)

Historical events were interpreted in the light of their respective faiths by the two communities. They tried to make sense of their victory and humiliation in defeat through reference to their faith. It was the faith that gave them explanations and direction. No wonder that the two strong identities and divine callings had to clash sooner or later. In the struggle for supremacy and survival—depending upon one's position at a given moment in time—that ensued as a result of their similar and contradictory visions, violent conflicts erupted from time to time. These confrontations often sucked the communities into the maelstrom of violence far from and within each other's borders. They caused a great deal of havoc. Blind retribution and consequent destruction of life and property ensued. Since no one power succeeded in imposing its rule by crippling or vanquishing permanently the other, the mayhem caused by what were viewed by their respective proponents as "holy wars" continued unabated. Even if they seemed to subside for a given period, their shadows hang in the air ready to engulf the region and the population once again on a killing and destructive spree.

In the fourteenth century, dissatisfaction has been brewing within the Muslim community who were scattered within enclaves that were separated from one another. The separation had been imposed by the Christian rulers. They pushed the Muslims to live in restricted areas. The Muslims on their part had been aiming at breaking out of these restricted areas and expanding their borders and influence far and wide. On its part, the Christian state had been strengthening its hand by expanding its borders. It had been increasing the pressure on the Muslim community and was marginalizing them as a result. The first but not the last strong clash of notice came in 1332 when a Muslim leader declared *Jihad* on the Christian state "invaded its territory, destroyed churches, and forced conversions to Islam" (Marcus 2002: 21).

Henceforth, clashes in the shape of "holy wars" became the order of the day. Christians and Muslims reciprocated by either initiating or retaliating in kind. Preservation and expansion by each party alternated one after the other. Population growth and environmental problems exacerbated the situation and led to more violent confrontations. In this early period, the relationship between Christians and Muslims in the greater region of the Horn of Africa began to assume an interestingly modern ring. Signs of tensions and collaboration between the adherents of the two faiths were in plenty. While the Christian state attempted to maintain its identity and jealously guarded what it saw as "its territory," there were varied reactions from the Muslim community.

Interestingly enough, there were sharp divisions within the Muslim community on how to relate to the other side. The community differed on the issue of coexistence on the one hand and holy war on the other. It was divided on what course to take. Marcus puts it as follows: "There has always been political dispute in Ethiopia's Muslim mini and microstates between pragmatists and zealots. The former chose to work with the Christian monarchy, whereas the latter preferred to spread the Prophet's word. In the early sixteenth century, differences between the two groups led to humiliating defeats (of the Muslims)" (2002: 31).

The seesaw between "pragmatists and the zealots" continued and manifested itself one way or another depending on the leadership that prevailed in the Muslim community. The internal bickering and opposing perspectives finally had their toll on them. They had the overall effect of weakening them. The internal conflict gave rise to the emergence of a party that pushed for the reassessment of the situation on the basis of the faith. Following such a disarray of the Muslims, a new and much greater confrontation was in the making. The Muslim side was strengthened and invigorated with the arrival of a powerful warrior.

AHMED IBRAHIM

Ahmed Ibrahim ("Gran," "the left-handed," 1506–1543) was a devout Muslim who hailed from the east of the country (Adal whose main city was Harar) raised by his equally devout kin. He was deeply disaffected by the plight of the Muslims. He found out that, on the one hand, the Muslims were living under the tutelage of the Christian state. From his perspective, this was unacceptable. On the other hand, the Muslims themselves had become impure. They had abandoned the strict observance of their faith. They had fallen from the pristine state and betrayed the principles of their faith. The internal degradation of the community and the external power of the enemy were two sides of the same coin. They had to be addressed simultaneously. Ibrahim had a double strategy. The first order of the day was the call for the purification of the community. Through his sermons and admonitions, Ibrahim created a strong and faithful following. There were many people who responded to his call for purity. Once he consolidated his grasp on the community, he turned his sight on the external enemy. The combination of internal reorganization on the basis of doctrinal purity and external enemy proved lethal and effective. They proved invaluable in galvanizing the community for a two-pronged cause. To counter the power of his enemy, "he proclaimed holy war against the Christian state…by whipping up a religious frenzy over the competition between Islam and Christianity. He declared a jihad" (Marcus 2002: 32).

Ibrahim was successful in his campaign. He overpowered the Christian state and broke off the isolation. For the first time, not only did he reclaim the periphery but also moved decisively and forcefully into what was often seen as the "core area" of the Christian monarchy. In the wake of this campaign, many churches and their possessions were destroyed. As the monarchy proved inadequate to match the strength of Ibrahim and his army, he extended his rule far and wide. The reaction to this humiliation by the Christians was typical of the consequences of a religion-inspired war: "[For] the Christian Highlands..., the Solomonic state reflected not only their inheritance but also their destiny. Chronicles about the time display not so much hatred against the Muslims as embarrassment that Christians permitted infidels to enter and devastate their country and holy places" (Ibid., 32).

In an interestingly modern twist, the two sides never shied from extending their call for help to their coreligionists outside their borders. Religious affiliations proved vital in the hour of need. When wars became fatal and defeat was in sight, the communities did not hesitate to call on a superior power that lay beyond their borders. The Muslims on their part were counting on "the moral and military support of the Ottoman Empire," which was flexing its muscles on the shores of the Mediterranean Sea. The Ottoman Empire had already extended its military influence to Egypt and Yemen.

There were far-reaching consequences as a result of the wars in this period. Islam began to expand and many converts joined its ranks. The Oromo also began to migrate northward in great numbers from the far south which they inhabited so far. Eventually, they became a strong force to be reckoned with. Not only were they becoming predominantly Muslim, but they were also instrumental in the propagation and expansion of the faith. As they adopted the Muslim faith in their droves, they increasingly posed a challenge to the state that defined itself as "Christian." For them, the adoption and adherence to Islam instead of Christianity became a badge of resistance. As a consequence of such a resistance, they declared *Jihad* on their opponents. The clashes between the adherents of the two faiths would become a part of the landscape in the region for years to come.

At the same time, other Oromos were gradually assimilated into and became part of the Christian state. "From the eighteenth century on, they became enmeshed in the political web of the country. The Gondarine rulers came more and more to depend upon their Galla (Oromo) troops, and the Galla (Oromo) nobility was an accepted feature in the Gondar courts" (Abir 1968: 27). This process was not always smooth because there were clashes here and there. Some of the battles proved bloody indeed.

Due to its victory as a result of the Portuguese expedition, the state also began to segregate Muslims intentionally. As the state got the upper hand, it introduced policies that restricted its Muslim communities in terms of residential areas and economic and social activities. In the mid-seventeenth century, de facto separation of Christians and Muslims was taking shape in some areas. Muslims were being confined to specific quarters even within cities and only permitted to practice some economic activities. They were prohibited from owning land and serving fully in government functions. In addition, what could be called "a culture of spiritual segregation" was gradually being introduced that marginalized further the Muslims. Toward the end of the century, they were given free but restricted space to express their religion and be ruled in their daily lives on the basis of its principles. They did pay their taxes, but they were administered by the *Sharia*. The case of the Muslims in Gondar is instructive in this case (Ahmed 1992: 102–116).

International developments also played their role in shaping the thinking of the monarchs. They had their influence in guiding their policies.

> To demonstrate the value of national unity, Tewodros had hoped to thwart and turn back Islam. As a man of the Western frontier, he had long been concerned with Cairo's encroachments…He was also keenly aware of the Turks, infiltrating slowly inland from Mitsiwa obviously en route to the highlands. That both threats to sovereignty came from Muslim powers fed the anti-Islamic prejudices that he had absorbed growing up. He regarded the record of Islam in Ethiopia as one of mayhem and subversion and concluded that his state was once again threatened by Muslim encirclement. He decided that alliance with the West was state salvation. (Marcus 2002: 69)

The fears of possible military conquest were not unfounded. Egypt took a decision to this effect and began to occupy the Eritrean coastland. Gradually, it moved south but was defeated in the first encounter. When a second attempt was made by Egypt, the confrontation was viewed naturally as a "struggle between Christianity and Islam." Luckily for the king, the Egyptians were defeated once again. The threat was not yet over. There was another attack coming from the west. The army of the

Mahdi (in Sudan) had moved east and occupied some areas. Here, there was a great deal of destruction when many churches were burnt and many Christians captured.

In their own way, in Harar, the British and the Italians had been itching for a fight to contain the westward expansion of Ethiopia. Harar was also brewing under the emir Abdullahi who was "a Muslim fundamentalist, who soon began persecuting European and Ethiopian Christians, forcing many to leave for Shewa and the coast" (Ibid., 83). The king of Ethiopia found a convenient excuse to send his army and attack the city. He did so easily and put his man in power that, on his part, fought his way into the Somali areas. By 1897, these areas had begun to effectively fall under the Ethiopian crown. In the course of the next ten odd years, the area was taken over by the monarchy. "Menelik (the king) certainly believed that his was a holy crusade" (Ibid., 104). Eventually, the Ogaden was recognized as part of his legal jurisdiction by the foreign powers that counted at that time. The annexation of the new area created a situation of rebellion in which the two faiths and their adherents began to clash.

During the reigns of Tewodros (1855–1868), Yohannes II (1872–1889), and Menelik (1889–1913), there were numerous campaigns against the Oromos which, by some estimates, constitute approximately 40–50 percent of the population of Ethiopia and approximately 70 percent of which were Muslims. In line with the history that has shaped this region, the campaigns were not only against the people as such but were also targeted as the adherents of a rival faith. In the course of the military campaigns, thousands of people were decimated, mosques burned, and many others displaced. Many more were forced to convert to Christianity. Even the leaders were not spared. The terror that was unleashed was on a grand scale.

In a too familiar scene, the routing of the Muslims was aided by the internal bickering and power struggles that took place within their leadership. The disagreements and factional fighting gave added impetus to the Christians to carry out their furious assault without any united resistance from their opponents. Destruction of the influence and reach of Islam, conversion of Muslims to Christianity, and the resultant strengthening of the state were the main aims spearheading the campaigns. After the extinction of any united front, the Muslim resistance continued with clerics scattered here and there. Some even connected their activities with those of the Mahdi in Sudan. Eventually however, their efforts could prove no match to the superior powers of the Christians who were using modern weapons.

During the nineteenth century, Muslims were also becoming more assertive and vocal. This trend manifested itself in what has been referred to as the "Islamic revival." It ostensibly had two aims: on the one hand, it was fighting the increasing power over and influence in their areas of Christians. These came, first, in the form of highland rulers. Ethiopia was expanding east and south into predominantly Muslim areas. This expansion was resented by a part of the inhabitants. Second, foreign colonial powers were making forays into the area. The Muslims in these areas used their faith to counter these external threats. They delved deeper into it and got inspiration from it. At the same time, their deeper studies and renewed engagement with their religion led them to devise new ways of social organizations, especially in the Somali areas. They began to find and practice novel ways of living together. These twin achievements led them further into a militant anti-foreigner stance. At the same time, they were engaged in missionary activities aimed at the non-Muslim societies in their areas. Even though they were looking outside, this did not in any way prevent them from looking inside as well. They also focused their attention on lax Muslims and called them to reform themselves by following strict piety on the basis of the principles of their faith.

LIJ IYASU

On the other side of the divide, another no less significant experiment was taking place. The new ruler in the area, Lij Iyasu, was a young boy of ten when he was designated the regent by his grandfather, Menelik, who was suddenly incapacitated due to a series of heart attacks. Iyasu was subjected to many palace intrigues beginning with the meddling of Menelik's powerful and ambitious wife, Taitu. The power struggles among the aristocracy also complicated matters. Even so, he managed to hold on to power through his deft machinations. Some of his opponents were imprisoned and purged. He distanced himself from his grandmother's position by removing those suspected of being her allies. He finally became the de facto king after the death of Menelik. He had to face a lot of problems. However, being so young and lacking a grasp of the complicated situation did not help him in the long run.

Even though he was young and unprepared for the huge task before him, he had entertained interesting ideas for his reign (Holcomb and Ibssa 1990: 145–170). He played with the possibilities of transcending the entrenched religious differences that obtained for many years and which restricted social and political life. The separation between Christians and Muslims had become a fact of life for many years. The new leader seemed, at least on the surface, to have dreamed of breaking down the barriers and creating a new society in which the adherents of the two faiths could live together harmoniously and even have a common cause (Pankhurst 2001: 205). It was an experiment that he was conducting that landed him in serious difficulties from the Christian side of the religious divide.

> Ethiopia's ruling class grew increasingly uneasy as World War I began, and Iyasu began a dalliance with Islam and also with the Central Powers. The heir believed that the defeat of the allies might allow Ethiopia to push Italy out of Eritrea and Somalia. He therefore sought an alliance with the Seyyid Muhammed Abdullah (d. 23 November 1920), the so-called Mad Mullah, who long has pursued an anti-colonialist war in Somalia. Since the Seyyid ipso facto followed an anti-Ethiopia line in Ogaden, many thought that Iyasu's policy was treasonous...His enemies...accused him of apostasy and [he] was excommunicated as an unbeliever and ended his abortive but interesting reign. (Marcus 2002: 114–115)

As Kapteijns points out, Iyasu's move was seen, at least by his detractors, as a part of a larger development sweeping the region. This was becoming attractive to local elements as well. Local movements in some areas in the region were raising their heads in revolt against the Christian authorities who were viewed as invaders. In their struggle, they drew inspiration and hoped for possible support and encouragement from other forces that were pointing to the same direction in foreign lands. From further a field, the Ottoman Empire had, before its demise, aroused strong pan-Islamic feelings. In its heyday, it was flagging signals of its intentions to impose pan-Islamic orders in areas far and wide. It had aroused some great expectations in this regard. Its sudden defeat thus came as a shock. Its defeat in World War I had created a great deal of resentment in pan-Islamist circles (Lewis 2004: xv).

Closer to home, from Sudan, the powerful Islamic movement unleashed by the Mahdi had also cast its shadow on this side of the border. It had in its own way aroused some sentiments that gave impetus to Muslim aspirations. Nor was the inspiration confined to the Mahdi. Closer still, the local revolts had contacts with elements that invoked and called for *Jihad* in Somalia. Coupled with all these trends, the direction toward which Iyasu was moving ruffled many feathers (Kapteijns 2000: 236).

SOMALIA'S *QADIRIYYA* AND *SALIHIYYA*

One also sees that the internal and external tensions were not confined to the Christians. While they were pulling each other apart and redrawing the political scene, their Muslim counterparts were also manifesting tensions that brewed within them. The two protagonists were the *Qadiriyya* on the one side and the *Salihiyya* on the other. Generally speaking, the former were open to cultivating constructive relationships with "outsiders" who consisted of the Christian rulers and the new colonial powers that were hovering on the horizon. They even went so far as to entertain collaboration with them. In other words, they were ready to interact with them and find common ground to work together on different levels. At the same time, they were also open to being more flexible as to include so-called non-Muslim practices.

> The Salihiyya, on the other hand, at least as interpreted by the Sayyid, insisted on militancy and holy war against both the Christian invaders and their Muslim associates...In Somalia, the jihad of Sayyid Muhammad (1898–1920) targeted local colonial collaborators, the tax raiders of Menelik's (the king of Ethiopia) expansionist state (overrunning western Somalia after the occupation of Harar in 1887), and the colonial administrations of British and Italian Somaliland...[with one] political ambition—that of establishing an independent Islamic state for Somalis. (Kapteijns 2000: 235–236)

The Sayyid who was in the forefront of the *Salihiyya* brotherhood is the darling of nationalists who see him as a forerunner of Somali nationalism (Bemath 1992: 33–47). Through his rabid anticolonial stance, he had stood against all foreigners, including the encroaching Ethiopians who were expanding their reach in the east. Somalia was reeling under the increasing pressure exerted by the colonial powers. There were some incidents that contributed to the overall dissatisfaction of the population. Such an atmosphere shaped him in his early days. One of the influences was some contacts he had with people close to the Mahdi in Sudan. The atrocities committed against the Islamic movement and the killings of fellow Muslims also had an impact on him. His *hajj* pilgrimage to Mecca also exposed him to pan-Islamist influences that were present at that time. There was a mounting awareness of the role being played by the Christian colonial powers that were viewed as threats to the Islamic world as a whole. Locally, education and cultural assaults by the newcomers that were impinging on the local population contributed to the anger that was boiling against the foreigners. The marauding Ethiopians had been sowing great fear among the Somali inhabitants. The Sayyid galvanized the population by the use of the faith and organized them into a resistance. Even though the Somalis were divided among themselves in clans and were often antagonistic to one another, he managed to make them overcome their differences and to create a united front.

It is interesting to note that the target of the Sayyid was not only the outsiders. He also cast his attention on the internal situation. He saw that his differences with the other brotherhoods, especially the *Qadiriyya*, were significant indeed. He condemned them for practices and beliefs that he believed were contrary to the faith. In some cases, he went even so far as to declare some of their teachings and practices as "heretical." He even admonished them to abandon their brotherhood and join him.

There were sharp divisions that were based on deep convictions. They sharply differed from their counterparts as to how to deal with what they saw and categorized as lax Muslims, those who were "a den of heretics bent on thwarting the faith." The *Salihiyya* were of the opinion that anyone who did not practice the pure faith as they preached it should be subjected to death. The same fate should be reserved to those Muslims who collaborate and fraternize with nonbelievers. Such Muslims were not different from unbelievers. Any semblance of assimilation and aping of unbelievers by adoption of their attire, participation in their gatherings, and any other manifestation of rapprochements to the infidels would render such Muslims apostates in their turn. Consequently, confrontation was the Sayyid's only option.

> The *jihad* was now, he (the Sayyid) argued, an inescapable Muslim duty in view of the fact that Muslims and Muslim lands have been tyrannized and brutalized by Christian invaders... The Sayyid branded Christians invaders, who remained fundamentally hostile to Muslims. Peace and prosperity could emanate only from God, the Qur'an and the Sunnah (the words and actions of the Prophet Muhammad). The Sayyid again severely criticized Muslims who maintained Christians as friends and collaborated with them. Muslims, he declared rather ominously, who associated with Christians should be subject to attack and should be shunned by other Muslims. The reference related to Muslims who served as guides to the Europeans, meaning the Somalis involved in the British Protectorate administration and the clans that now had vested interests to maintain under British protection. (Bemath 1992: 45)

The *Qadiriyya* on their part were not at all prepared to accept the position of the Sayyid. As a matter of fact, they insulted him as one who was out of his mind and was not sober. In their turn, they accused him of distorting Islam. They were of the strong opinion that he was misinterpreting it. They hurled the accusation of heresy at him. They did not stop there. They reached the point of accusing him of rowdy behavior. They criticized him for being bent on disturbing the peace that was slowly gathering pace. Unless his activities were curbed, they reasoned, he would create havoc in the long run. To this end they approached the British and advised them to take the necessary measures to arrest and silence him. Others went so far as to chase him from their area of control.

The heated exchanges show that, in this case, there was a strong disagreement going on for the soul of the faith among its concerned adherents. In the first place, the doctrinal differences were very sharp. They were so vehement that each party was accusing the other of sliding away from the true religion. For instance, Sheik Uweys of the *Uwaysiya* "inveighed against his rivals as 'incestuous' apostates" and judged "*Qaadiriyya*'s ancient tenets as heretical" (Samatar 1992: 54–55). Second, in their search for purity, the *Salihiyya* brotherhood scoffed at any act of borrowing anything suspected of being foreign. This group adhered to and recommended a strict interpretation of the teachings of Islam. Not only was any cultural aspect that smacked of foreignness rejected; any association with the infidels was also vehemently condemned.

The *Qadiriyya* on their part did not see any problem in working with foreigners. They interacted with them freely and joined and collaborated with them in the administration of the country. To the chagrin of their coreligionists, they contributed their share in what they saw was a positive development in the country. In the event, the sharp divisions reached fever pitch. The coreligionists could not see eye to eye. There were even incidences of physical clashes where some people died. Were it not for the presence of the foreigners who served as a buffer zone as it were between the two factions, a serious conflict would have erupted. A civil war was averted only by the mediation of what were seen as "the *kaffirs*," at least by one section. In this case, the "unbelievers" were both sources of the intensive conflict and a blessing in disguise in averting it. The conclusion drawn by Bemath is ominous indeed:

> In summary, had it not been for the presence of the French, British, Italians, and the Ethiopians, who were seen as common enemies by the

Somalis, this religious and doctrinal dispute might have created a large scale rift between the two *tariqas* (brotherhoods). In view of the deep doctrinal antagonism between the two *tariqas*—and the consequent ill feeling generated among their devotees—it is no wonder that the Somalis in the closing decades of the twentieth century were not plunged into a disastrous internecine blood letting based on religious discord, and possibly civil war. (1992: 45)

The amazing thing is that the rivalry and contention that characterized the two brotherhoods are not history yet. They still exert their influence at present. The followers of Sheik Uweys still cherish the life and teachings of their leader. In what Samatar refers to as a "legacy of bitterness," they still remember his death as martyrdom in the hands of enemies, "members of a 'satanic faction,' the *Saalihiya*." They meet every year in the place of his burial and engage in powerful celebrations. They undergo deep spiritual experiences. In fact, the influence of the Sheik extends as far as Tanzania and there are adherents of the teachings of the Sheik far and wide.

ISLAM AND SOMALI IDENTITY

The contribution of the Sheik goes further. According to the analysis of Samatar, the contention between the Sayyid and the Sheik Uweys reflects the attempt to define the very core of Somali identity. Following the late Somali President Shermarke, Samatar argues that Islam is at the center of the Somali identity. It is one of the pillars that defines the essence of what a Somali is, the other being poetry. It goes further: it is the basis of the Somali national consciousness. Islam and nationalism are intertwined. Therefore, based on the argument of Samatar, one could safely draw the conclusion that the definition and clarity on the meaning of Islam is crucial to the identity and life of Somalis. On the one hand, it is imperative that there is a consensus on the interpretation of Islam. Such a consensus has far-reaching consequences for the Somali people. On the other hand, if there is a discord on this very crucial issue, then there are bound to be dire consequences. In the absence of such a consensus, there cannot but be a fissure in the polity.

Samatar argues that Islam and poetry answer the Somali question of "who are we?" If Islam has such a central role in the definition of the Somali identity and nationalism, it follows logically that the relationship between the *Qadiriyya* and the *Salihiyya* brotherhoods takes one to the core of the Somali psyche. The untrammeled antagonism and outright hostility manifested one against the other becomes a life and death struggle to define "authentic Islam" and, by extension, to claim the essence of being an "authentic Somali." The stakes are very high indeed! The daggers are drawn in a sensitive and dangerous way (Samatar 1992: 64–65).

The repercussions of this theological and doctrinal controversy and its effect on Somali nationalism and identity are still strong. It seems that the rupture between the two brotherhoods had brought the Somali people to the brink of a violent confrontation. On the one hand, the rabid anticolonial militancy of the *Salihiyya* only contributed to the death of thousands of people. Their opposition to the occupation powers, however worthy it might have seemed, only succeeded in causing considerable havoc. Not only were many lives lost; there was a great deal of material destruction. In retrospect, the *Jihadists* only managed in causing irreparable damage.

Further still, the fact that one brotherhood felt it religiously permissible to kill a member of another brotherhood professing allegiance to the same faith for the sake of the preservation of the purity of the faith speaks volumes about the extent to which the parties had drifted far apart. It also witnesses to the fact that a sword was driven into the Somali soul that threatened to tear it apart. All accounts agree that the ominous result of it all would have been a violent and bloody confrontation. The resultant destruction would have been unimaginable for the Somalis. Had such a confrontation taken place and the militants had the upper hand and vanquished their enemies, what would have been the short- and long-term consequences? Samatar is not sure of the positive benefits that would accrue from such a victory of the militants. Perhaps the Sayyid would have instituted "an autocratic theocracy," in the words of Samatar. Many opponents would then have taken up arms against him and his rule. With no trace or inclination to compromise with his opponents in his behavior and never disposed to giving concessions to those who disagreed with him, the prospects for a peaceful coexistence between the brotherhoods would have been unthinkable. There would have been room for nothing else except for the sword. The result would have been fratricidal destruction of considerable proportions.

WORLD WAR II

In the years that followed, religion also played a central role in the rest of the Horn. The Italians and the British were flanking Ethiopia on two sides. They had found a foothold on Eritrea and Somalia. There were two opposite scenarios being played out in this period. On the one hand, the local populations were opposed to the Christian invaders, whatever their place of origin. Faith was a strong incentive and gave the ultimate guidance in the choice of an enemy and a friend. The Oromos in the mainland and the Somalis were also up in arms against those they saw as the intruders. Their calls to resistance and opposition were on the basis of their faith. On the other hand, the colonial powers were determined to weaken Ethiopia by encroaching on what it was slowly claiming to be its territory. The colonial powers were slowly but surely doing everything in their power to undermine the extending reach of Ethiopia. When it came to World War II and the invasion of Ethiopia in 1935, the religious flame was rekindled.

For Muslims, the Italian occupation of Ethiopia provided them the opportunity to express themselves more forcefully against the Christian dominance. Many of them, especially Somalis, were recruited in the Italian army that was fighting the Ethiopian state. Many of them also sided with the Italians and gave them significant and valuable support in their effort to weaken the Ethiopian resistance. To this end, the Muslims were given more freedom in the exercise of their religion by the Italians. They were permitted to build mosques, run educational institutions, and practice the *Sharia* and use Arabic widely, especially in newspapers. The Italians also introduced administrative measures to strengthen and unite Muslim dominated areas in the country. Pilgrimage to Mecca was permitted. On his part, Haile Sellassie was playing the religious card as well. He urged his compatriots to "fight for their national existence and their religion, without which they would be like the serfs of Somalia and Eritrea" (Marcus 2002: 142). Religion and war were thus intertwined in the name of people and country.

This trend continued even after the war. When Sellassie returned to the throne, he reversed many of the gains that were registered by Muslims under the Italian occupation. The Muslims were increasingly discriminated against on a number of levels. They were restricted in owning land and serving in government institutions. Their collaboration with the enemy had generated ill feelings on the part of the monarchy. The cumulative effect was that the feeling of marginalization fed the flames of war. The Muslim dominated areas of the country were up in arms. The Somali areas especially became a thorn in the flesh of the monarchy.

To make matters worse, the idea of forging "a Greater Somalia" consisting of the Ogaden, northern Kenya, Djibouti, and the Italian and British colonies was being pushed by the British. In the process, their plans and efforts to bring this idea to fruition instigated and energized the Somali Youth League (SYL, formerly, Somali Youth Club [SYC]) (Barnes 2007: 277–291). The idea sent jitters down the spine of Ethiopia.

Even when Somalia became independent in 1960, the religious rift and pan-Somali nationalism was feeding war plans. When Oromo and Somali areas found a reason to revolt against the central government, Mogadishu picked it up and began to fan the flames. Once again, the message from the city was couched not only in political but also in religious terms. "Broadcasting to both groups, Radio Mogadishu stressed the need for Muslim unity against the Amharas" (Marcus 2002: 178). When the growing tensions escalated into a war with Ethiopia in 1977, religion was still at the center. Even though the Soviet communists had sided initially with Somalia, which had expressed allegiance to socialism, and Ethiopia was also a Marxist-Leninist state, no one could ignore "the passionate issues of religion and nationalism that characterized international relations in the Horn of Africa" (Marcus 2002: 178).

ERITREA

In Eritrea, the political temperature was rising with the abolition of the federation by the Ethiopian government. Eritrea had been an Italian colony since 1896. When the Italians were defeated by the allies in World War II, Eritrea was taken away from the Italians and given to the British under a mandate from the UN. Even in this initial stage, the issue of religion was not far from the surface. During the era of the British administration, numerous campaigns on the future of Eritrea were mounted. On the whole, people were divided on religious lines. While a part of the population advocated for the reunion of Eritrea and Ethiopia, the other half advocated immediate independence. Roughly speaking, it happened that the unionists were mostly Christian highlanders while those opting for independence were lowland Muslims. In the event, there was much antagonism between the two parties. In some cases, they were inclined to use violence against their opponents. As Meredith puts it, there was no question about the fact that it was not only nationalism but also religious affiliation that divided and influenced the parties, which were divided on what step to take: "Eritrea's future proved difficult to resolve...Arab countries proposed an independent state. The Eritreans themselves, numbering about 3 million, were divided over the issue. The Christian half of the population…tended to support unification with Ethiopia. The Muslim half of the population…tended to favour independence" (Meredith 2005: 208).

The division based on these two antagonistic visions and aims continued in one way or another in the years ahead. The various opinions on the issue could not be reconciled. They became deeply entrenched in the course of time. When the British left in 1952, Eritrea was "federated with Ethiopian under the Ethiopian crown" under a resolution of the UN. In 1962, Ethiopia unilaterally abrogated the federation. Eritrea was joined to Ethiopia.

The party favoring independence took a decisive step in 1960. A number of people from the region came together and founded the Eritrean Liberation Front (ELF). At this stage, there were a number of factors that elevated the religious affiliation of the founders. As David Pool observed, "ironically, divisions between Muslims and Christians, their different relations to the Christian character of the Ethiopian imperial order, and the different socio-economic levels of the regions they inhabited, had been factors which precipitated the armed struggle and initially confounded it" (Pool 1998: 21).

There are three important factors that may be noted in this connection. First, the establishment of the front took place in a foreign country. The members of the new rebel movement were based in Cairo, Egypt, at the time of the launching of the ELF. The Arab connection could not be missed at this juncture. Second, it was also brought about by a part of the group on one side of the dividing line. A majority—if not all—of them also happened to be Muslims. Third, at this stage, the movement was couched in Islamic terms. It presented itself as Muslim inspired movement and tried to appeal to the Muslim/Arab world for support and financial aid. Eritrea was being presented as a country inhabited by a Muslim population that had been sucked into a Christian state against its will. Even the Eritrean People's Liberation Front (EPLF), the rival group which eventually overwhelmed the ELF affirmed and argued that "the ELF based its struggle on Islam and Arabism." Gradually, however, people from Christian highlands joined the rebel movement and changed radically the landscape. Through their socialist and Marxist political orientation, they created a new and unifying dynamic during the period of the fight for liberation. In the process, however, the shadow of religion managed to tear the independence movement apart.

The influx of mainly Christian highlanders into the movement had a profound effect on its organization and direction. Religion was slowly edged out of the ideology and socialist theory got the upper hand. As the opposition to the ELF grew in strength, there was no place for compromise. At a time when the Ethiopian assault was becoming formidable and the two movements had the possibility of forming a united front against the enemy, they fell out and began a fratricidal war. The predominantly Muslim ELF and the scientific-socialist EPLF engaged in internecine war in 1972. Their differences were only resolved when one of them, the ELF, collapsed under the EPLF assault in 1981. The war caused great human and material damage and contributed to the unnecessary delay in the acquisition of Eritrean independence.

The repercussions would also be felt for years to come. One of the unforeseen outcomes was that a variety of Islamic groups proliferated. Even though their numbers were few, they had initiated movements whose aim was the establishment of an Islamic state in Eritrea. They were fragmented on what course to take to bring this about. Some of them collaborated with the National Islamic Front (NIF) in Sudan and opted for armed struggle to attain their goal. They even launched sporadic military forays against Eritrea. Their fortunes would of course often depend on the Sudanese-Eritrean relations of the day. Some of them chose to follow a nonviolent path and distanced themselves from bellicose statements and postures.

AFTER WORLD WAR II

In Ethiopia, Muslims found a new voice when the monarchy was overthrown and the military government took over in 1974. They were emboldened by the change to pursue their interests and put forward proposals. Even so, there were some obstacles. As Marcus puts it, "in recent history, the state has been identified with the Semitic-speaking, Christian population, and since World War II, specifically with the dominant Amhara culture. For the non-Christian, non-northerner, the cost was assimilation into an alien culture" (Marcus 2002: 219). If the armed movements in the Oromo and Somali regions are to be taken as proof, such a possibility has been resented and even rejected. On the whole, there was a mood of disappointment in some quarters regarding the place of Islam in the country. This was expressed by one disgruntled Muslim writer in 1993: "Despite its having a Muslim majority, the world knows Ethiopia as a Christian country. The Muslims of Ethiopia are the most unhappy section of the world Muslim *Ummah*...They are persecuted at home by Christians and are utterly neglected by their co-faithful inhabiting the Muslim world."

In the 1990s and well into the beginning of the twenty-first century, the religious contestation in the region did not abate. On the contrary, it found new expressions through a more militant mood. As Gill Lusk puts it, the takeover of Mogadishu by the UIC "also brought Islamist politics, which sent alarm bells ringing within Somalia itself and in neighbouring Ethiopia and Kenya, not to mention nearby Arab countries...Ethiopia felt that it had much to fear from the Islamists in Mogadishu: it has long experience with its own Islamist rebels, including the Sudan-backed OLF, and with the Islamist government in Khartoum" (2007: 26–29). In this light, the opinions expressed by two Ethiopian scholars are pertinent indeed. Bahru Zewde writes, "Wise and prudent leadership is required on both sides (Christian and Muslim) to make sure that these two old religions do not abandon their tradition of mutual tolerance (except for one epoch, i.e. during the wars of Ahmed Gragn) and pursue a path of bloody conflict...Many observers are worried lest Ethiopia, successively subjected to the stresses and strains of class struggle and ethnic conflict, becomes an arena of religious warfare" (2002: 10). Similar opinion is expressed by Alemseged Abbay: "In addition to ethnicity, another primordial element, religion, hitherto latent, is emerging as a potent source of identity. Gradually, it is becoming Ethiopia's newest polarizing factor" (2009: 194).

Throughout the Horn, militant expressions of Islam are manifesting themselves in greater strength and boldness.[1] Armed confrontations have become the order of the day on many fronts. In many instances, this goes hand in hand with increased religious consciousness that has contributed to a renewed sense of identity. This is also fed by Pan-Islamic resurgence beyond the borders of the Horn. The free flow of ideas and material assistance has its share of influence on the region. On their part, the governments have woken up to the challenge in their own ways. The situation that prevails in Somalia is one of the developments that contribute greatly to the religion-based turbulence that has engulfed the region.

CHAPTER 6

VIOLENCE AND ISLAM'S CHALLENGE IN SOMALIA

ONE OF THE INTRIGUING DEVELOPMENTS REGARDING THE ROLE OF religion in violent conflict and the ambiguity of the holy warrior/infidel is Somalia. It is interesting mainly for two reasons: first, it has evolved an insurgency that is fuelled by religious convictions. This is taking place in a context where the population is religiously homogenous. Somalis are predominantly Muslim. Generally speaking, their adherence to and advocacy of a state run under a radical Islam was not visible earlier in their history. In fact, for the greater part of their life as an independent country, the state was mostly more secular than religious. The dominant ideology under Siad Barré was socialism. Consequently, Muslim leaders who did not tow the line or challenged the state were severely persecuted. As Somalia disintegrated in the wake of the fall of Siad Barré, however, the Islamic option increasingly became viable.

Second, Somalia becomes interesting because of its regional implications. Mainly because of its geographical position, Somalia straddles the Arab and African divide. Just as Sudan, it is a member of the Arab League as well as the African Union. The people of Somalia also claim to be of Arab descent. Its effect as a meeting ground or confrontation of the two entities (African and Arab) cannot be underestimated. It is an open secret that the two forces are engaged in one way or another in the conflict. Religion and race thus become players in the arena.

SOMALIA AND ISLAMIC WORLD

A journalist/columnist in one of the Kenyan daily papers, Mr. Salim Lone, has, on several occasions, addressed himself to the issues of conflict and peace especially as it concerns religion. He has in a number of articles highlighted the dangers that the Horn of Africa region is facing. He has written about the conflict in Somalia and its regional and global implications. Even though he seems to simplify matters, uses facts selectively, and argues from a certain perspective,[1] his overall conclusion that there is a danger that should be addressed is a point well taken. Let us quote some of his statements in this regard as an entry point:

> The world has never been so unstable or threatened. With Somalia invaded, the world and our region are even more so, with four countries now occupied, all of them Muslim... The whole region could be engulfed by this crisis... The same global paralysis and despair that could not prevent the ongoing Iraqi holocaust must not now be allowed to let Somalia unravel... Inaction now will surely see the Horn of Africa become an even bigger powder-keg. (Lone 2007: 11)

For Mr. Lone, the ascendancy of Islam in Somalia especially in the shape of the short-lived Islamist administration is part of the new worldwide resurgence (what Prof. Mazrui calls "revival" not "radicalization") of Islam. He relates the seizure of power, however brief, by the Union of Islamic Courts (UIC) in Somalia in 2006 to that of the gathering strength of Islamists in other parts of the world. He writes,

> Islamists are now fully part of the mainstream in all Muslim societies. Their parties are powerful presences in a growing number of countries, including Sudan, Iran, Palestine, Pakistan, Somalia and Egypt. Political Islam is here to stay. Most of its followers can live comfortably with the West, but will not accept dictation from the West. Suppressing them is a recipe for disaster. Co-existence is the safest route for us all. (Lone 2007: 11)

For Mr. Lone, there is a sort of conspiracy to oppose or suppress all movements that have to do with Islamists globally. This is not an idea to which he is privy. This idea of "a Muslim world under siege by external forces" is shared by many Muslims, not only Osama bin Laden. Regarding Muslims in East Africa and elsewhere, for example, Prof. Ali Mazrui says, "There is a greater articulation of domestic discontent and also an articulation of the global grievances of the Muslim world... the disproportionate use of military power against non-compliant Muslim states. So there is more anger than there has been for a while, about those issues, but nowhere near a full-scale intifada, a domestic uprising against local oppressors even if they are African governments, or Al Qaeda, which is an international orientation of such a rebellion" (Smith 2007: 45). Locally, for instance, according to Mr. Lone, this bias has been demonstrated in dealing with the Islamists in Somalia. "Even though the Courts were primarily a moderate Muslim union, the offspring of businessmen, they nevertheless were vilified in the build up to war as extremists" (Lone 2007: 11). Vilified, they were then subjected to an illegal invasion by the (Christian) Ethiopians. Not only were the latter supported in this act of aggression by the (Christian) United States; they were also indirectly encouraged by the neighboring states. He expresses his worry that such a bias may also operate in this region with states with a majority of Christians. In his opinion, this would lead to a very dangerous confrontation. A different approach must be tried. Such opinions show how the case of Somalia has its place and meaning in a larger and wider context.

SOMALIA IN THE BEGINNING

Compared to the majority of African countries that gained their independence in the so-called winds of change of the 1960s, Somalia had a number of things going for it. From the start, there were three characteristics that were special to Somalia. First, it had one religion: Islam. Second, it had one language. Compared to many other African countries, this was special. Third, other than a small minority of Bantu origin—approximately 6 percent, who initially are said to have come from Tanzania—the ethnic origin of the population was homogenous. Somalia, as David Lamb says, was "blessed with ethnic uniformity... Unlike most other Africans, the 4 million people of Somalia are fiercely nationalistic. They share a common language and a common culture and a common belief that their Moslem leaders are descendants of the Aquil Abu Talib, cousin of the Prophet Mohammed" (Lamb 1987: 11, 197).[2] This was perhaps the reason why Somalia became a member of the Arab League as far back as 1974. Even though they were divided into many clans and subclans— and this proved to be fatal in the long run—they could claim to belong to the same "racial" stock. Again, compared with other African countries, the advantages were huge in Somalia. Somehow, the advantages simply failed to add up and to deliver at the hour of need. This is an enigma that baffles friends and foes alike!

If one looks at the history of Somalia, one learns that religion was important indeed in the life of the people. As we saw in the previous chapter, it played an important role in fashioning the identity and the life of the people. Islam also became at times a rallying means for their resistance against foreign invaders. Even so, the significant thing is that religion was never a defining element in the formation of a united polity. It did not at any point become a factor in the formation of an all-encompassing state, as was, for example, the case with Ethiopia. Religion was indeed an important factor in the societies in this region. For instance, the Christian-Muslim tug-of-war was a recurrent feature in the history of the region. However, at no time did Islam become a political tradition on the basis of which an all-embracing administrative polity was formed in Somalia.

SIAD BARRÉ

This background did not deter Siad Barré from challenging Islam. For whatever reasons, he introduced a socialist regime and ruled the country on that basis since he came to power in a 1969 coup. In the first few years following the takeover, he dallied with Islam. He seemed at first to want to bring on board some religious leaders who were intent on bringing their religion to bear on public life. The rupture came when he introduced reforms that did not consider their sentiments. As a result, there was serious opposition to his rule from some of them whom he suppressed brutally. He even executed some *Imams* (religious leaders) and imprisoned others. Some of them fled abroad and tried to organize resistance to the regime.

EMERGENT UIC

It was especially when the state begun to collapse in 1991 that the religious alternative became a possible option. Slowly but surely, Islamist groups began to mushroom here and there. They were filling the vacuum that was left by the disappearance of the state. Each in their own ways, they were attempting to respond to the challenges that life without a state posed. They were trying to cope with the anarchic situation by applying what they know best and was close to them, namely, Islam.

In the course of time, a number of Islamic groups came together under the banner of UIC and changed the landscape. They were initially opposed by a coalition of warlords who had been the bane of Somalia ever since the fall of Siad Barré. They had divided Somalia among themselves. They managed their respective areas and made a lot of money through extortion, taxation, and by managing the seaports and the airports. They manned the notorious checkpoints that separated their artificial borders. They engaged in fierce battles whenever a warlord moved to the area controlled by another. They had their own clan militias that served their bidding. Somalia was thus hopelessly divided.

It was only when their survival was threatened by the growing power of the UIC that the warlords decided to form a coalition. According to some observers, they were allegedly goaded and supported by the United States. There are reports that they were provided with millions of dollars to form a united front with the goal of stemming the tide of the Islamists. To everybody's surprise, including themselves it seems, the UIC routed the warlords. Most of them fled from the onslaught. For the first time since the escape of Siad Barré, Mogadishu and some parts of Somalia were effectively under one administration free of the hitherto ubiquitous and all-powerful warlords.

Even though they themselves were surprised by their victory and were not prepared for the new task that suddenly lay before them, the UIC went ahead in imposing the *Sharia*, took some administrative measures, and restored some kind of order. They undertook harsh steps against those who went against their laws and regulations based on their understanding of the *Sharia*. In this manner, they succeeded in bringing relative peace to the country. The airport and the port were opened; the much-detested checkpoints were removed. People could move freely. Many saw that Somalia was on the way to stability and reconstruction after so many years of chaos. Many began to rest their hopes on them. Some even spoke of the "Mogadishu miracle." This is how one report presented the situation:

> The Courts expanded between June and December 2006, bringing a degree of peace and security unknown to the south for more than 15 years. Mogadishu was reunited, weapons were removed from the streets and the port and airport reopened. By December, the Courts had expanded from their Mogadishu base to control most of the territory between the

Kenyan border and the autonomous region of Puntland in the north-east…Communities seemed prepared to tolerate a strict interpretation of Sharia law in return for peace and security.[3]

Mr. Salim Lone was full of admiration and defiance:

> They [the UIC]were not angels, but they performed some remarkable miracles in bringing peace to most of Somalia and driving out the warlords. They did not commit a single terrorist act. They made some miscalculations, but…the Courts were never going to be a client regime in Somalia. (Lone 2007: 11)

One of the most positive presentations of the UIC and their accomplishments was made by Prof. Abdi Samatar of the University of Minnesota, USA.[4] In an article that he wrote after a brief visit to Mogadishu in June/July 2006, he painted the rule of the UIC in glowing terms and predicted a better future for the country as a result of what they had accomplished so far. There are a number of themes that figure in his article, which are significant and which contribute to the discussion on Somalia.

First, the Somali conflict has two antagonists: the local and the international. On the local level, the antagonists are divided between the warlords and the UIC. In contrast to the UIC, the warlords are "the merchants of violence" who had destroyed the country. They had taken the people hostage and subjected them to their evil intentions and machinations. On the international level, the international community spearheaded by the United States and Ethiopia has supported these warlords against the wishes of the people and prolonged the mayhem and destruction. Second, Many peace initiatives have failed mainly because of the negative intentions and influences of foreign actors. The latter conspired and aborted the peace processes that could have served the will and the wishes of the Somali people for reconciliation. The warlords continued their rule only because they were supported by outside powers that scuttled any attempt at reaching a peaceful resolution. The tactics of the outside world consisted of imposing its solutions on the people. This is the case, for example, of the reorganization of the warlords into a council. Such a council was an arm of the outside world and did not have the interest of the people of Somalia at heart. It became a tool of the "war on terror" that had its adverse effects.

The establishment of the Transitional Federal Government (TFG) in 2004 also strengthened this trend. "The international community blessed the imposition of a government of warlords on the Somali people" (p. 1). By establishing the TFG, the Horn of Africa regional body, the Inter-Governmental Agency for Development (IGAD), and the international donors that brought it into existence were simply going against the will of the people of Somalia. They were imposing an "illegitimate" body on the country. The machinations of Ethiopia, which played a very vital role in this and other peace processes, were crucial and decisive in convincing the other actors.

Third, a new force was gathering pace as the warlords continued their campaign against the people. The UIC was becoming a new force to be reckoned with. In a hitherto unforeseen confrontation with the warlords, the UIC suddenly and unexpectedly had the upper hand. This victory was due to the unequivocal support it enjoyed from the people. "The public rallied overwhelmingly behind the courts." The UIC reflected the will of the people. Consequently, the UIC "liberated the population of Mogadishu and the surrounding communities in July 2006." One of the strong positions maintained by the UIC and the people was opposition to the deployment of foreign troops in Somalia. The coming of the UIC exposed the weaknesses and the incapacity of the TFG, "the Ethiopian Trojan horse" (p. 6).

Once the UIC won, they were surprised by two things: first, they were not mentally and organizationally prepared to deal with the complications of the world they forced themselves into. They "neither had the education nor the work experience to manage and administer national or regional institutions" (p. 3). Second, they came to power suddenly without any such expectation. They were not equipped to deal with the responsibility of reestablishing and running a state. The only instruments at their disposal were the *Sharia* and fierce opposition to foreign involvement, "particularly Ethiopian and their IGAD allies" (p. 4).

Whatever their weaknesses, the fact is that due to the triumph of the UIC, there is now a new reality in Mogadishu and parts of Somalia (while under the UIC). The new situation has been created by the van-guard of the UIC inspired by Islam. "The uprising of the Somali population in and around Mogadishu led by the Union of Islamic Courts has created the best chance for peace for the city and the country" (p. 6). This new situation has come about through the "the people's revolt and its leadership." As a result of these new developments there is no doubt that "freedom is in the air" (6). The people-supported UIC have now the upper hand and have created a space full of new possibilities for the first time after sixteen years of mayhem. This position is supported by others who see the UIC as the genuine representatives of the opinion of the people. "Contrary to conventional wisdom, the Islamic Courts do not derive their power from military power alone. This is a popular movement that is riding the crest of a xenophobic wave that has swept the country. The Islamists enjoy wide acceptance and respect, and are viewed as vanguards against Western influence."[5]

According to Samatar, the challenges for the UIC will consist of focusing on the local and the external. On the local level, uniting a fragmented society and refocusing it on issues of local and national interest will be a priority. The UIC and the people have one positive factor at their disposal: "the public's confidence in the Islamic faith is a major asset that should be strategically deployed to facilitate this effort, namely, mobilizing the population for reconstruction" (p. 5). Since Islam as a faith was instrumental in vanquishing the dreaded warlords, it has also the sole capacity to bring the people together for a common cause. It was "the common Islamic faith that brought the people together." Islam was the force behind the challenge posed to the warlords and their supporters and their eventual demise. It can now offer the rallying point to the population. In fact, in the face of the dangers that will come from outside, "the UICs has asked the Somali population to be prepared *to wage war against invaders* and their Somali supplicants,... a war inspired by Islamism and nationalism" (p. 7, italics in the original). The UIC is a new wave that is challenging the unholy mix of local warlords and foreign forces. "The Union of Islamic Courts (UIC) rose to power in late 2006 to counter this and brought a relative peace to the capital during its six-month reign" (Samatar 2008: 35).

On the international level, the UIC have to find a mechanism whereby they can respond to the accusations and attacks hurled at them by forces allied to the "war on terror." Both Ethiopia and the United States in cohort with the TFG are identified as the primary culprits here. They are by all accounts the most immediate threat to the new found liberation and are intent "to destabilize the peace brought about by the triumph of the UIC and undermine the possibility of re-emergent Somalia that is united and independent" (p. 6). The only option for the UIC is "to galvanize the population in order for them to defend their new freedoms" (p. 6).

The euphoria underlying the article is understandable. The basic thrust of Prof. Samatar's argument is that there is a clear division between what the Somali people want on the one hand and what the international community is trying to impose on them. The people's will in this case is represented by the UIC-inspired and led Islamism coupled with Somali nationalism. The Muslim faith is thus at the center of the changes. It follows that this will be one of the main factors that will be instrumental in creating a new order of peace and reconstruction.

The problem with such a one-sided argument is that it simplifies a very complicated conflict-ridden situation. Many questions come to mind. To wit, are the Somali people so united and speaking with one voice? Have all the clan divisions that had wracked the society for the last sixteen years vanished in one sweep with the appearance of the UIC? Have even the majority of the people rallied behind the UIC as one man? Was the TFG the sole creation of outsiders without involvement of the Somali people? Is the international community, including the neighboring countries, alone the culprits and to be blamed for the chaotic situation that reigns in Somalia?[6] Is the Islam that is said to be the force behind the UIC and the Somali people one version which is not contested? In other words, is there only one interpretation of Islam that dominates the scene and united everyone under it banner? These are some of the questions that may be raised by the article. From the look of things, there are many who will not be convinced by such a black and white picture.

To begin with, the religious situation is more complicated. According to some observers, the UIC was not united even ideologically. In other words, it was a mixed bag that had not thought out clearly and even unified its religious stand. The various components were divided sharply when it comes to the currents of Islamic thinking. There were different and conflicting strands. "Far from being a monolithic force, Somalia's Union of Islamic Courts (UIC) is heavily divided along ideological lines" (Abdi 2006: 27). On the one hand, there were what are often referred to as the "radical" and "moderate" wings (Barnes and Hassan 2007: 155). Among the former are those who advocate the strict interpretation of Islam. "The Salafists favour a rigid and literal interpretation of Islamic texts and regard other Muslim sects as deviants. Salafis teach against compromise and holy war is the pivot around which their beliefs revolve." Their radical interpretation had led them to antagonize parts of the society. They had even gone so far as to behead people on the basis of strict *Sharia* law, closed cinemas even those showing football matches, banned musical broadcasts as being contrary to Islamic teaching and practice, closed radio stations, and even "stormed wedding parties and mixed sex gatherings."

Furthermore, there are those who are more moderate in line with traditional Islam practiced by Somalis, which is said to be tolerant. This is more of a Sunni inclination that promotes more of individual contemplation and piety. As a result, "the traditional mainstream Sunni sects are creating their own Islamic courts in a bid to counter the influence of the UIC." One opinion has it that, when the Ethiopians attacked the UIC, the "moderates" abandoned the radicals to their fate when they thought that the radical wing went too far. According to this opinion, the "moderates" were ready to approach the TFG to find together a middle ground. The fact that they "refused to fight" had played a decisive role in the eventual defeat of the UIC (*Economist* 2007: 33). In the long run, once the honeymoon is over, the UIC would have had their opponents, even those who would oppose them violently. Taking such differences within the UIC into consideration, the view of a London-based Arabic publication is critical indeed:

> The price of ignoring the "Afghanisation" of Somalia will be costly. The national interests of nations such as Saudi Arabia and Egypt will be threatened...The Islamic courts are an extension of the Salafist-Takfiri (ultra-puritans who consider other Muslims as apostates) forces which do not recognize the legal boundaries of states. They will not hesitate to set the world ablaze, subdue it by the sword and impose their own vision of what they see as Islam.[7]

This view on the boundaries of states is supported by two aspects of the UIC. The armed wing of the UIC do not hide the main aim for which they are fighting. First, the so-called Al-Shabaab is bent on implementing the dream of "Greater Somalia." This is meant to say that all the people of Somali origin who now live in Ethiopia, Kenya, Djibouti, Somaliland, and Puntland would be incorporated into a unified state comprising all Somalis in the Horn. Second, once all the Somalis are brought together under one roof, they would be ruled and administered under strict *Sharia*.

Naturally, these twin aims have sent shivers down the spines of neighboring states. Consequently, just as there was praise of the UIC from some circles, alarm bells were also ringing in others. Views were sharply divided on the Islamists who took over Mogadishu. Some were even expressing the fear that a "Taliban-style" regime was in the process of being formed (Mbuvi 2007: 10). The religious divide was drawn as sharply as never before!

Unfortunately for them and their supporters, the UIC committed a number of errors that exacerbated the situation. First, their sudden success over the warlords gave them a false idea of their strength. They began to see themselves as invincible, ready to face any opponent, and subjugate it militarily. There were also many others who saw them in this light. The reference was always to "the powerful Islamists." Second, they began to play the Islamist card. Other than imposing *Sharia*, they made clear their intention of extending their influence further, including the neighboring countries. Their alleged or suspected connection with foreign Islamist movements also drew the attention and eventual apprehension of other countries. They were being accused of having connections with international terrorists and even the al Qaeda network. Some even went so far as to allege that they were harboring terrorist elements (Khalif 2009: 18).

JIHAD AND CRUSADE

One thing that raised the stakes higher was the UIC declaration of *Jihad*. Once they did so even on Ethiopia, the situation took a religious dimension that put on edge many a country. It raised the question of whether a decisive and far-reaching religious confrontation was taking shape in the region. If this took place, it would be a new development that would change the nature of the Somali conflict. The UIC began to criticize the neighboring countries, specifically, Kenya and Ethiopia. They questioned the neutrality of Kenya and refused to meet there for negotiations with the TFG despite the long involvement of Kenya in the Somali peace process. They preferred instead Khartoum as the venue and the Arab League as the mediator. In this way, they showed that they were not thinking in regional terms and they rejected their integration in it. By taking such a route, they may also have been raising the religious flag a little higher. Worse still, they revived the pan-Somali vision of incorporating the Somali-inhabited parts in the region. In their unguarded moments, they became increasingly belligerent and even threatened to march to Addis Ababa, issuing an ultimatum of seven days. In their initial aim of gaining control over all Somalia, they were inching slowly toward Baidoa, the sit of the TFG, surrounding it and ready to take it by force (Oluoch 2006: 16–17). The cumulative effect of it all was that a major confrontation seemed to be in the offing. Charles Onyango-Obbo puts the finger on the point:

> Now the Islamists have declared holy war against Ethiopia. At the same time, to the extent that there are Arab-radical Islamic forces active in the Horn and northern Africa, they must have taken the peace settlement in Southern Sudan as a great loss. Apart from oil, this is the reason the Khartoum government has taken a hard line in Darfur…Informed diplomatic sources allege that in this bigger Arab-Islamic battle against what is seen as a concerted attack from the West, they too have decided that Somalia is where the definitive battle will be fought. There are claims of Egyptian and Libyan military elements working with the Courts. (2006: 12)

The UIC's call for a *Jihad* did not go without any response from outside Somalia. The Ugandan President Yoweri Museveni is said to have responded forcefully. In the words of Ismail Omar Guelleh, the president of Djibouti,

> Uganda paints the situation (in Somalia under the UIC) as a conflict between Christianity and Islam and is preparing to launch a crusade in the Horn of Africa. President Yoweri Museveni refers without any constraint to a holy war. He has stated that he will take appropriate action to the end that what happened to the Islamists of Hassan El Turabi in the Sudan will also be the fate of the Somali Islamists. (Ouazani 2006: 84, my translation)

The temperature had gone a notch higher. The most worrying aspect was that the political and hitherto limited interclan infighting in Somalia was taking a dangerous bend. It was increasingly assuming all the trappings of a conflict fuelled by religious convictions. At the same time, it was transgressing the borders and threatening to spill over into the neighboring states and involve them in the conflict. It seemed to be inching toward replicating the north-south divide that had operated in the Sudan. This time round it was not confined to a limited border but was going beyond it. It was threatening to involve more nations; it would become international in its scope. This would also sharpen the already delicate racial and religious fault line that was increasingly manifesting itself in the Sahel—Chad, Niger, Mali, and the Sudan—that was referred to earlier in connection with the discussion of the situation in Sudan. The prospects were ominous indeed for the region that has its own share of other problems to deal with!

It happened that the UIC were chased out of power in December 2006 by a combined force of the TFG and the Ethiopian army. There is ample evidence to show that they are still a force to be reckoned with. They are still a powerful element in the country. The Islamist component is still there. Only the future will tell what their effect will be on the region. There are a number of elements that should be taken into consideration in this regard.

First, as pointed out earlier, Somalia just as Sudan is a bridge between black Africa and the Arab world. One observes that it is torn between its allegiance to the black African south and the Muslim/Arab north. It is not clear as to where it should look for direction. This dichotomy in the identity and psyche of Somalia is amply evident in the politics and policies of the various leaders. There was a fissure that could not be easily overcome.

This fissure begins with the choice of the venue and the mediators in the dialogue. On the one side, the UIC was opting for the mediation of the Arab League. It was pushing the idea that it was the League that should spearhead the negotiations between the parties. The UIC pushed for the idea that Khartoum serve as the venue of the negotiations. The UIC was more inclined to participate in a negotiation conducted under the aegis of the Arab League. We had earlier seen that Somalia had become a member of the League in 1974. By such a move, the UIC was sending the clear signal that its Arab connection was to be taken seriously. Interestingly enough, there was also the religious side as well. Second, the UIC was shunning Kenya that had been involved in the search for the solution to the Somali crisis more than any other country in the region. The ostensible reason for rejecting Kenya as a venue as well as an honest broker was that it was viewed by the UIC as having compromised its neutrality by supporting the TFG and the Ethiopians.

Meanwhile, a new opposition group consisting of remnants of the UIC met in Asmara, Eritrea and formed the Alliance for the Re-liberation of Somalia (ARS). A new and vigorous attempt was made to reconcile this faction and the TFG by bringing them to the negotiating table. It was conducted by the special representative of the UN Secretary-General to Somalia, the Mauritanian Abdullah Ould Dada. While the TFG and the Asmara group were inching ever so slowly toward a possible agreement, there was a split in the latter. One party participated in the negotiations that were taking place in Djibouti. The other refused to recognize it. Finally, an agreement was reached to merge the TFG and one of the factions of the ARS. In fact, a former leader of the UIC, Sheik Sharif Sheik Ahmed, was elected president in the election that took place after the signing of the peace agreement.

There is an interesting side to the negotiations. It was programmed that after the successful end of the negotiations, the negotiators would go to the Muslim holy place of Mecca to sign the agreement. The choice of Mecca as the most appropriate venue for the signing ceremony could be that, in the light of sixteen failed agreements, no chances would be taken for another failure. The force of Islam would be called upon. The religious card would be the ultimate guarantor to avoid failure. "After the initialing in Djibouti . . . the next stage is to be a full signing of the accord by both sides in Jeddah, Saudi Arabia, and the signatories will then go to Mecca to sign on the Koran to demonstrate their public commitment" (Smith 2008: 48). The Arab and the Muslim connections assume a great deal of importance even in guaranteeing the solidity of the agreement.

Lastly, the connection between the war in the Sudan and Somalia could not be ignored. By some estimates, there is the view that the war in Darfur is an extension of this war against the West. This will include other Christian states, especially in the region that are suspected to be supporting the West. As one observer puts it, "The tension in the region allows Sudan to pursue its own complex and Islamist agendas . . . Led by Egypt, Arab states (like Somalia, Sudan belongs to the Arab League) have kept quiet, swallowing Khartoum's propaganda line" (Lusk 2007: 29).

FISSURE IN THE SOUL?

On the whole, there is an intriguing side to the conflict in Somalia and its persistence. In this light, questions abound. Many are searching desperately to find an explanation. In an interesting analysis of the reasons behind the Somali civil war, two Somali writers have offered two possible explanations of the conflict in Somalia. The well-known Somali writer Nuruddin Farah sees the conflict as resulting from the incompatible visions that obtained between what he referred to as the "urbophobics" and the "urbophiles," those who hate and love the city, the rural and the urban mentalities that are opposed to and suspicious of each other. The incompatibility of the two finally led to a rupture. According to Farah, the city of Mogadishu used to be a cosmopolitan meeting point for people of various origins and backgrounds. The two visions—the rural and the urban—could not coexist. At one point, the rural invaded the urban and contributed to the destruction of the social fabric (Farah 2005: 13).

Abdulkadir Khalif on his part says that the source of the conflict lay in the fact that the Somali people have been torn between two poles (Khalif 2005: 15). One pole, the "regional bloc," is disposed to accept the status quo, namely, the separation of the Somali people in various countries—Somalia, Kenya, Ethiopia, and Djibouti. In other words, it is at home with the idea of accommodating itself to the principle of the Organization of African Unity (OAU) that recognized the inviolability of colonial borders. The other pole, the "anti-regional bloc" espouses the unification of the scattered "Somali nation" into a unified state. The dream of "Greater Somalia" that was part of the original five-star flag that was adopted at the time of independence from colonial rule remains the symbol of this group. They believe that "the Somali nation" is indivisible and should be brought together. This was the vision that inspired Siad Barré and led him to a devastating war with Ethiopia in 1977 (Tesfai 2006: iv). This is also the vision being espoused by some sections of the UIC. As Khalif states, the tension was prominent early and even lead to the assassination of the late Shermarke in 1963 (2009: 18–19).

Be that as it may, there is another profound source of contention. The previous pages have shown how Islam is at the center of the Somali identity. A number of Somalis have forcefully expressed this conviction. They argue that it is only through the unifying power of Islam that the country would overcome its problems. If so, the question arises as to what interpretation of Islam would bring it about. Still, others agonize over this point: "In the light of the fact that Somalia is the only country in the whole continent whose population is virtually all Muslim," Mohamed

Haj Mukhtar asks, "What is there in Islam to foster murder, rape and starving to death of one's Muslim brethren?" (1995: 1–2).

The dilemma becomes stark when one considers the positions taken by two powerful personalities of the Somali scene. A very crucial development in this connection is the separation of the two central figures in the UIC: Sheik Sharif Sheik Ahmed and Sheik Hassan Dahyr Aweys. Both were prominent in the UIC before its ouster. They formed the ARS together in exile. At a certain stage, they parted ways. With their public pronouncements, it may be said that their interpretations of Islam play key roles in their separation. They reflect their interpretations in their support or opposition to the "regional" (Sheik Ahmed) and "anti-regional" (Sheik Aweys) approach. They both accept *Sharia* but disagree on how to implement it. This is a crucial stage indeed. "Questions that immediately come to mind are: Which madhabu, or school of Islamic jurisprudence, will serve as foundation for legal practice?" (Goldsmith 2009: 10).

The views of Sheik Sharif are interesting in this context. There are at least five important aspects of his position as the new president. When considering these aspects, one has to look at the history of Somalia in the last two years since June 2006 when the UIC had the upper hand. There are repercussions in these developments that are important to our argument.

First, former enemies, namely, TFG and ARS (Djibouti) agreed to bury the hatchet and walk together despite their differences. The Islamists and the "secularists," those who advocated the establishment of an Islamic state under *Sharia* law and those who adhered to the "constitution" that regulated the Transitional Federal Institutions (TFI) came together. The former chairman of the Islamist group was eventually elected head of this hybrid entity. It is true that the parliament based on the TFI finally resolved that *Sharia* become the law of the land. For the moment, this is an oxymoron. Only time will tell how this concoction will work out in practice.

Second, right after his election, the new president went to Addis Ababa, Ethiopia, to take part in the African Union summit of heads of state and government. The man who headed the "enemy camp" and was attacked by the Ethiopian troops and chased away from power was received in what was recently viewed as an "enemy territory." From the diehard Islamist perspective, opposition to "outsiders" and "unbelievers" is an article of faith. Collaboration with them is opposed vehemently.

This time round, Sheik Sharif had taken a different path. It happened that in both the AU and the IGAD meetings, the two former opponents accepted each other and sat together in one forum. That was a significant step in itself.

Third, Sheik Sharif brought Islam into the center of the discussion. In the process of bringing stability to Somalia, Islam will play a role, he asserted. He starts from the understanding that the various belligerents have contradictory perspectives on Islam. In his opinion, this conflict is a question of the interpretation of the faith. He argues that some groups have adhered to a wrong interpretation of the faith. Various Islamist groups have even declared "holy war" against each other due to such misinterpretations of the same faith. Some, who were part of the UIC outfit, such as Hassan Dahyr Aweys, have even vowed to oppose him as the new president based on their understanding of the faith. Sheik Sharif recognizes this state of affairs and declares the need to address it. He even goes so far as to say that "those fighting to impose a strict version of Islamic law throughout the country had misinterpreted the religion and he would try to correct that."[8] In other words, the interpretation of the faith, in this case, Islam, is right at the center of the violent conflict that is ripping the country and the people apart.

Fourth, the only way to peace is to approach one another and put the faith on the table as it were and argue one's case. The way forward is to engage all the factions in a serious dialogue regarding the specific interpretations of the faith to which they adhere and make reference to in connection with their projects and courses of action. In a very interesting move, Sheik Ahmed even proposes that Islamic scholars be brought in to shed light on the faith and everything related to it in the Somali context. In this way, the faith and all its interpretations are brought to the public square and debated. There is no question that this is a fascinating way forward.

Fifth, Sheik Ahmed goes further. He vows that he is willing to stretch one's hand of peace to "outsiders." He expresses the opinion that the West and Ethiopia are frightened when they hear the term *Sharia*. They need not be, he argues. Even in the past, Somalis had often resorted to Islam in the administration of their daily lives. There is nothing new in this regard. If need be, he expresses his willingness to go the extra mile to explain the meaning of the faith to others. Even during his UIC days, he is quoted as saying: "We did not bring any new form of Islam to Somalia; but if the West has particular issues which need clarification, especially about the application of Islam, we are ready to explain our agenda and how we will go about it" (Oluoch 2006: i, iv, v). In his line of thinking, both the local and the international have the need to engage the faith and the faiths in an open and transparent discourse in the public square to the end that the respective interpretations and understandings of all concerned are clarified and misinterpretations corrected.

Such moves do not seem to stop the rupture or contradiction on the interpretation of Islam and the vision of Somalis. Undoubtedly, it is still there.

> His (Sheik Shariff's) opponents at home accused him of abandoning the Islamist agenda and compromising the principles of an Islamic state in Somalia in favour of a secular government. Sheikh Hassan Mahdi, spokesman of the Islamic Party accused Sheikh Sharif of abandoning his ideals. "Sheikh Sharif and his followers have abandoned the noble idea the moment they merged with the regime of the *Murtadeen*." *Murtadeen* is Arabic for those who abandon Islam. Sheik Sharif's supporters reject the idea that they are sell outs to secular politicians. They neither accept the notion that secular politicians are *Murtadeen*...Radical Islamists...insist that the Koran and the citations of Prophet Mohamed constitute the only pillars of an Islamic state in Somalia...The stage is set for further confrontation as eastern African states under the auspices of IGAD push for more (10,000) peacekeepers even as Al Shabaab and the Islamic Party view them as heathen occupation forces. (Khalif 2009: 18–19)

Considering these developments, could one then exclude the possibility of a return and/or a replay of scenes that rocked the Somali society at the beginning of the twentieth century discussed in the previous chapter? At that time, the division between the *Qadiriyya* and the *Salihiyya* was bitter. In the event, the disagreement concentrated on a contradictory vision based on incompatible interpretations of Islam. The two groups were vehemently opposed to each other. They went so far as to accuse each other of heresy. They saw each other as deviations from the right path of Islam. Could it be that the lessons that could have been drawn from this period have been lost? Or could history be replaying itself? Would one also be right when one suggests that the fissure would heal only when a unified Islam is put on the table and shared by all parties? There seems to be no doubt that there is the need for an internal and external public square where the different interpretations and visions are thrashed out in a spirit of give and take.

Unfortunately, the stage is not yet ready for such a meeting of minds. Tragically enough, the war of interpretations is being waged on the Somali battlefield with all its concomitant horrors. The unresolved ambivalence of the holy warrior/infidel will continue to cause havoc to the Somali social fabric. It will only subside or be resolved to the satisfaction of both the "insiders" and "outsiders" through the encounter of all concerned in the public square.

CHAPTER 7

INITIATION INTO PEACE

THE PREVIOUS CHAPTERS COVERED SITUATIONS WHERE RELIGION GAVE
rise to violent conflicts. From south to north, from west to east, religion
provided the rationale for violent conflicts and wars. Even so, one should
be careful not to draw the conclusion that religion was only instrumental
in causing violent conflicts or wars. There are other equally forceful religious responses such as the quest for peace. To have a balanced view on
both, it behooves one to see the African in one's relationship to religion.
The propensity to violent conflicts and the search for peace must also be
seen from this perspective. It is only when one explores the relationship
of the African to religion that we can situate the entire discussion in its
proper context.

As far back as the end of the sixties, the Kenyan theologian John
Mbiti made a significant statement about the religiosity of Africans.
In his book, *African Religions and Philosophy*, the writer claimed that
Africans were religious through and through; they were religious to the
core. In his own memorable words, he wrote,

> Africans are notoriously religious, and each people has its own religious
> system with a set of beliefs and practices. Religion permeates into all the
> departments of life so fully that it is not easy or possible always to isolate
> it. A study of these religious systems is, therefore, ultimately a study of the
> peoples themselves in all the complexities of both traditional and modern
> life... Because traditional religions permeate all the departments of life,
> there is no formal distinction between the sacred and the secular, between
> the religious and non-religious, between the spiritual and the material
> areas of life. Wherever the African is, there is his religion... Although
> many African languages have no word for religion as such, it nevertheless

accompanies the individual from long before his birth to long after his physical death...In times of crisis they often come to the surface, or people revert to them in secret...In their traditional life Africans are deeply religious. It is religion, more than anything else, which colours their understanding of the universe and their empirical participation in that universe, making life a profoundly religious phenomenon. To be is to be religious in a religious universe. (Mbiti 1994: 1, 262)

Subsequent observations have corroborated the earlier statement. Numerous other studies have shown that it is difficult if not impossible to think separately of the African and his religion. This does not of course limit one to the two universal religions, Christianity and Islam. African Traditional Religions are also part and parcel of the religious environment. One also observes that the religious faithful are adept at holding on to a religious potpourri that brings together various elements from different sources.

SECULARISM VERSUS RELIGION

During the post-independence period after many African countries gained their independence or when they were conducting armed struggle against colonial powers, many leaders were inclined to move away from and shun religion. They mostly espoused the Marxist-Leninist or socialist philosophy especially as liberation movements. The leadership was composed of elites who had been mostly educated in foreign universities. They were also steeped in the communist teachings of Marx, Engels, and Lenin. Consequently, they subscribed to the atheistic philosophy following or echoing Marx's dismissal of "religion as the opium of the people." Most of them were either benevolently indifferent to religion or vehemently opposed to it. They introduced strict so-called scientific socialism that relegated religion to the backwaters of society.

Some among them were even working toward the eventual eradication of religion. True to their mentors, they were also convinced that religion was on the way out. Over against religion, a hard line secular ideology held sway over the society. Some, such as the TPLF, whose victory led to the formation of the current government in Ethiopia, were adherents of a diehard Albanian communism even in a sea of very religious people. They were part of a wave that was spearheaded by the educated minority. They all professed some sort of Marxism/Leninism deemed progressive and all-encompassing philosophy. It gave them all a readymade recipe for changing radically the societies in which they saw backwardness and underdevelopment. The common denominators that tied them together, among other things, were "Marxism, secularism" (Young 1998: 36–38). At one time or another, there were communist/ socialist parties in Angola, Guinea, Ethiopia, Namibia, Mozambique, Somalia, and Sudan—to just name a few. The buzzword was "revolution," and revolution could only be carried out through a "scientific socialist" worldview that excluded religion. On the whole, the leadership was convinced that a secular path to development was the order of the day and that religion belonged to the ever dwindling and disappearing past.

Even those who professed profound Christian convictions at least in public were not devoid of such a decidedly secular leaning. Kenneth Kaunda of Zambia was used to professing his deep attachment to Christianity in public. This did not prevent him from referring to himself as a "humanist in Africa." The revered first president of Tanzania, Julius Nyerere, was himself a devout Catholic. He was a member of the church throughout his life. He is even being recommended to be named a saint by the Catholic Church after his death. In his socialist experiment, touted as "Ujamaa, family hood," one of his intentions was to place not God but man in the center. In West Africa, as in many other parts of Africa, "the new elite in control of power opted for a secular order" (Kaba 2000: 191).

RESURGENCE OF RELIGION

The landscape has now changed radically; religion is back in the open. In retrospect, one wonders whether there was any time when it did not exercise its power, overtly or covertly. As Mbiti had argued so forcefully, religion was always a power to be reckoned with in Africa even in the face of fervent allegiance to secular ideologies. Africans breathe religion. The brief dalliance with scientific socialism did not have a permanent root or impact. It never succeeded in affecting profoundly the overall picture. With the collapse of the Soviet Union and the subsequent discredit of communism as a viable economic and social theory, the trend fell into desuetude. A residue and relic of some leadership's commitment and nostalgia to such a philosophy only remains in the attachment to the "liberation movement era" or with some few states still adhering to communist ideology.

It is perhaps in the light of these secular beginnings that dwindled away in the course of time that Patrick Chabal and Jean-Pascal Daloz speak of the "re-traditionalization of Africa" (1999: 63–76). They argue that Africa is becoming more and more traditional in its everyday life. This consists in people being immersed in religion, including the occult and what is usually referred to as "witchcraft." Every aspect of life is explained by religion—poverty, wealth, illness, wellbeing, development/underdevelopment, death, among others. The game of politics is no exception. For example, no politician in his right mind would dare ignore the power of religion to affect one's capacity or otherwise to have access to or seize power. One would only ignore it at one's peril. It follows that many who aspire to public office have to rally on their side or employ the best religious leaders or medicine men and women to enable them to reach the goal and beat any competitor in the process. A recent story from Nigeria illustrates how essential these kinds of rituals have become:

> Nigerian police have arrested a witchdoctor employed by a politician to perform rituals at an election tribunal, local media reported today. Officers caught Oluwole Abiodun on Wednesday at the court building in south western Ondo state with charms and copies of the Bible and Koran in a black plastic bag. A pot containing a rabbit, seven eggs, cowrie shells and palm oil was found nearby, the state news agency of Nigeria said... The witchdoctor's rituals would have been intended to ensure that the challenge to the election of the legislator failed.[1]

Strangely enough, this infatuation with religion goes hand in hand with what is called the rational. Many tools and signs of modernity accompany this religious outlook. Regarding the political arena, for instance, the politician would readily preach democracy, the rule of law, elections and balloting, as well as the justice system. All these systems are more or less built on human rationality and logic. There is no divine or spiritual explanation or cause behind them. They are products of human beings putting their heads together. Contemporary African politicians and compatriots believe that one can influence the results of all these systems through the right manipulation of the spiritual realm. The complication and complexity inherent in such a position is stated by Mohammed Salih when he wrote about the leadership of Sierra Leone as follows:

> The Mende elites who dominated the state were very secular in their political orientation. Their adherence to traditional secret societies as an

instrument for controlling state functions, despite centuries of Christian missions is still a puzzle for many observers. The social life of the Temne, with their Muslim connections, is equally dominated by tradition and custom rather than of the practice of their Islamic faith. (2001: 119; Geschiere 1997)

As Salih shows, there is an unlikely mix of a number of disparate and seemingly contradictory elements. For a rational point of view, they do not belong together. Salih argues that, normally, the practice of traditional rituals should not sit comfortably with either Christianity or Islam. However, politicians do not see anything strange in the art of mixing two seemingly opposite things. In this sense, one can mix the "secular" and the "religious." One also sees no contradiction in adhering to the universal and the traditional religions at one and the same time. The aim is to get maximum benefit by mixing everything together. Such people may present a secular picture to the outside world. They may publicly profess to uphold the tenets of modernity by giving allegiance to a secular order. In secret and deep inside, however, they put themselves under the sway of religious forces that can be manipulated by experts of the spirit world. The end result is the achievement and maintenance of power. It is in this light that Chabal and Daloz write:

> Whatever the political condition of Africa today, there is no doubt that religion is thriving. The facts cannot be denied: Africans are deeply religious; the realm of the irrational is growing, not diminishing; and religious beliefs or cults have become politically critical...There is ample evidence that witchcraft remains central to the lives of most Africans, including Christians and Muslims. (1999: 69, 73)

Stephen Ellis and Gerrie ter Haar have developed this perspective in their book, *Worlds of Power: Religious Thought and Political Practice in Africa* (2004). They argue that the African may only be seen and understood through the religious prism. To the African, the meaning of everything that takes place in the world has to be extracted through religion. It can only be understood and explained through religion. There is no sphere in life that is out of reach of religion. It follows that daily activities and occurrences must be conducted under the shadow of religion.

To live one's life, the African has to submit oneself to the phenomenon of religion. In this chore of living life, one relies on the experts, the high priests, and priestesses who can see into the twilight zone. By getting the necessary reading of the course of one's life and acquiring the appropriate advice, one is assured of handling one's life and controlling it to one's benefit. This includes the volatile area of politics. Ascending to a position of power and acquiring subsequent wealth demands that one is in control of immense spiritual powers. One has to have the religious means to manipulate all the forces to attain one's goal. Success in this endeavor attests to the fact that one has found the right religious formula. Failure to succeed shows that another person with more powerful tools has stolen the success. Successes and failures are thus explained in religious terms. There is no separation between the spiritual and the mundane. This religion-dominated worldview of the African world is finding resonance with the global resurgence of religion.

On the global scene, religion has been in the eye of the storm. This is in sharp contrast to the situation that prevailed in the recent past. There was a time in the sixties and the seventies especially when religion was confined to the realm of the irrational. The general prediction was that religion would once for all be confined to oblivion. As secularism progressed irrevocably, it was taken for granted that religion would gradually be relegated to the periphery of life and would cease to have any influence on life in general and politics in particular. Secularism would have the upper hand and sweep the world taking the place of religion.

Gradually, however, it has been recognized that religion has become a very potent force in the world. Religion is back with a vengeance (Huntington 2005: 359). It has reemerged as a powerful element in the private lives of a great majority of the world's population. Moreover, its role in influencing society is growing by leaps and bounds. Consequently, this phenomenal change is being studied in depth. It is being acknowledged that religion has also become a significant player in the political arena. Unfortunately, its ugly side in fomenting and perpetuating sometimes reckless violence is becoming prominent as well. Religion has now become a potent factor in contributing actively to conflict and peace. Its potential for both has now been acknowledged. As a result of the resurgence of religion, there are now many studies that are devoted to the role of religion in conflict and peace.[2]

This role of religion cannot be ignored when dealing with Africa. The influence of religion extends far and wide. This goes hand in hand with the fact that religious leaders are a highly respected group. In comparison to other leaders in society, they are the group that stands out as being in an extremely special position. They are accorded a high degree of trust.

In this connection, the result of a recent survey is interesting and illuminating indeed:

> The survey (commissioned by the BBC World Service and Gallup International Service) found out that across Africa, religion played an important role with religious leaders as the most trusted group. A good 74 percent of Africans trust religious leaders, with more people (72 percent) wanting to give them more power than any other group. Feelings for religious leaders are particularly strong in Nigeria, with 85 percent trusting religious leaders and a similar number keen to give them more power. Politicians in Africa, as in the rest of the world, are the least trusted. (Agutu 2005: 21)

With this in mind, one has no difficulty in arguing that one can understand the African mainly in religious terms. Religion imbues the everyday life of the African. Even the political arena is not devoid of religion. It does not operate independently of religion but is influenced and guided by it. Religion is the lens, as it were, through which politics and daily life are viewed. Life in general is interpreted and made sense of through religion and politics is no exception. Ellis and Ter Haar put it as follows:

> We contend that it is largely through religious ideas that Africans think about the world today, and that religious ideas provide them with a means of becoming social and political actors. The study of religious thought therefore constitutes a privileged opportunity for observing political practice in Africa... Religious thought needs to be studied seriously if we are to understand politics in Africa today. (2004: 2–3)

RELIGIONS FOR PEACE

It is in this context that one should place the projects of religious leaders and the faithful work for peace. They operate within this environment to address politics with the goal of achieving peace. They have noted the devastating effects of wars and violent conflicts. They have measured and weighed the human and material costs that are caused by wars. They have thus reached the conclusion that their religious faith is not a source of violence and wars. The wars that are waged in the name of religion in fact, they argue, distort and misinterpret the fundamentals of the faith. Rather than being a source of war, religion can be and is the source of peace. They are convinced that the faiths they hold can be used to attain peace. It is the aim of this chapter to explore this topic and to see what the contribution of religion has been in the subcontinent in enhancing peace.

To begin with, Africa is richly endowed with religious pluralism. When one looks at the religious map of the continent, one observes that there are indeed a variety of religious affiliations that adorn it. According to the statistics, there are a variety of religious groups in many countries of the continent (Barret 2001). Even though there are religious majorities in some countries, one sees that pluralism is a character of the subcontinent as a whole. Only in very few cases can one speak of religious homogeneity. One should also assert on the basis of the evidence that despite the religious heterogeneity that is there with all its colors, there is on the whole a tradition of peaceful coexistence among the various religious groups. Ellis and Ter Haar put it as follows:

> In general, there has been rather little violence on religious grounds in African conflicts, even where the population is thoroughly diverse, including Christians, Muslims and others. Violence organized along religious lines is most closely associated with Sudan and Nigeria... Properly speaking, there are no religious wars in Africa south of the Sahara. (2004: 107)

This is a bold and encouraging statement to make especially considering the global trend of fundamentalist extremism, which has contributed much toward the polarization of peoples on the basis of religious differences (Kepel 1994). There is no reason to doubt that such an environment where religious differences live side by side without clashes obtains in sub-Saharan Africa at present. Among the many examples is the case of Senegal (Stavenhagen 1996: 187–191).

However, one wonders in the light of recent developments for how long this view will hold. We have seen earlier how polarization and differing visions of religion are increasing. In the long run, one cannot exclude the possibility that they may contribute to violent conflicts. It is also a question of how long the places so far unaffected by religion-based conflicts will stand the tide, especially the global one. One notes that the general trend of religious extremism is also unfortunately characterized by the hardening of contradictions based on religious convictions. This is the trend much popularized by the theory of "the clash of civilizations" (Huntington 2002).

When we considered the role of religion in the incitement of violent conflicts, we focused on a number of countries that had suffered such problems. One also observes that, apart from the prominent religion-inspired violent conflicts and wars, there are also minor ones that have not hit the headlines in a big way. This is the case for instance when one looks at the conflicts in the Democratic Republic of the Congo (DRC) and other minor conflicts that have affected some regions in Africa like Guinea In such cases, religious sentiments and affiliations become the basis for the engagement in violent conflicts that shatter the social peace. Keeping all this in perspective, the rest of the chapter now turns to deal with the role of religion in the construction of peace. It will focus on the efforts aimed at stopping, winding down, and resolving violent conflicts. It will look at the peace building efforts expended by religion and its leaders.

When one looks for such examples, one finds out that such efforts are not new. On the contrary, one finds that some intrepid people of faith have been applying themselves to the task of seeking peace. In the midst of violent conflicts that raged with ferocity, they were practically the only ones who had the courage and capacity to face the challenge to address the belligerent parties and earn their respect. Even though the circumstances that prevailed at a given time were not conducive to their efforts, they showed sheer determination based on the faith they held.

One could mention many places in sub-Saharan Africa where religious groups made a difference in situations of violent conflicts. There are a number of places where attempts have been made or are being made to address the situations of violent conflicts from the perspective of faith. The chapter will only take a few of the initiatives that have made headlines. It needs to be pointed out that there are also smaller but significant initiatives that take place without attracting the public attention they rightly deserve.

MOZAMBIQUE

Let us start with the role of the churches in the process of bringing peace to Mozambique at a great risk. The peace process was a triumph of the art of bringing together a variety of actors to work for the same goal. The first initiative was taken by the Rome-based Community of St. Egidio, a group of Italian Catholics who apply themselves to addressing and resolving conflicts wherever they occur. They were initially approached and assisted by a local priest, Dom Jaime Gonçalves, who later became the bishop of Beira (Van Tongeren, Brink, Hellema, and Verhoeven 2005: 576–581). The initial aim of the first meeting was to find ways and means of easing the pressure of the communist regime in Mozambique on the churches. It gradually saw a bigger picture of its role.

Since its independence from Portugal in 1974, Mozambique was caught up in a civil war that pitted the governing FRELIMO party and the opposition rebel movement RENAMO. The war was bloody by all standards. Millions of people were displaced and thousands killed during the conflict. There was no end in sight even though many groups tried their hand to bring about peace. When they could not succeed, the small community ventured into the scene. Before embarking on the peace process, the community had laid the ground for the peace initiative through various activities aimed at building confidence with and among the warring parties and the areas under their control. The confidence building measures also consisted of visits to Rome by the leaders of the factions, provision of humanitarian assistance to the victims of war, and opening up discussion channels with all parties, among others.

In 1989, all the activities matured into the launching of the peace initiative proper. The local churches on their part were not idle, especially the Catholic Church. For instance, the pastoral letter of the church urged and admonished that peace be pursued. "There must be an end to war," said Cardinal Alexandre, the Archbishop of Maputo in the Pastoral letter of April 15, 1990. "[There must be] reconciliation between Frelimo and Renamo, and the arms which massacre the people must be silent" (Alden 2001: 13–33).

This courageous call to peace in the face of opposition from the government was a follow up to the one made in 1987. The latter had opened the door to the possibility for negotiations even though it had enraged the government at that time. Still, it succeeded in placing the church as a neutral body that could deal with both parties to the conflict. To this end, the various churches in the country tried to bring their resources and energies together. "Central to the process of instigating negotiations between the two protagonists was the role played by the Catholics and Protestants through the Mozambican Christian Council (CCM). The Institutions had, despite deliberate campaigns by the government aimed at subverting their position in society, maintained a strong following among ordinary Mozambicans" (Alden 2001: 13–33).

The change of guard after the death of Samora Machel, the fiery first president of Mozambique, opened a new window of opportunity. The new leader, Joaquim Chissano, saw the situation in a different light. He came to the recognition that there was no military solution to the conflict; he was open to consider a political solution. At the same time, he began to move away from a strict "scientific socialist" worldview to introduce capitalist economy. The West was providing much needed humanitarian aid that encouraged economic and political change. The government also changed its hitherto hostile relationship toward the churches. It returned confiscated land to the churches and opened up space for their various activities, including educational and health services. A new era of cooperation was introduced. These moves brought about further possibilities for nonpolitical actors, especially the faith-based organizations (FBOs), to make their mark. Slowly but surely, they were able to convince the government to follow the way of peace and to open the line of negotiation with the main rebel group. The peace agreement was finally signed in 1992.

More had to be done to consolidate peace and strengthen it. The CCM became very active in devising programs that supported the peace process and took it forward. They focused primarily on the issue of disarmament (Van Tongeren et al. 2005: 623–629). They collected many firearms that were still in the hands of former fighters. Incentives were offered to make them part with their weapons, which were then destroyed to prevent any possibility of reusing them. The scraps were in turn used to make works of art that strengthened the establishment of peace. At the same time, they tied this exercise with the goal of inculcating a culture of peace in the population at large.

It seems that the work of engagement for peace never comes to an end. When there is good news from one side, there is also another challenge on another side. While the religious leaders were expressing satisfaction with some results, another front opened up with the possibility of conflict. And the leaders are called upon to address it:

> Religious leaders in northern Mozambique are making attempts to prevent an outbreak of communal violence after three mosques were burnt in a matter of weeks in Lichinga, capital of Niassa Province... The incidents are highly unusual in Mozambique, where religious tolerance is the norm.[3]

SUDAN

Another example of the search for peace is the Sudan. The country has often been associated with endless wars since its independence. There are also examples of attempts to address the conflicts from the FBOs. To begin with, churches in Sudan were very much involved on various levels during the war especially in advocacy (Sudan Ecumenical Forum 2003). They took it upon themselves to inform the outside world about the plight of their people. They were also engaged in alleviating the suffering of the people through the social services they offered. These consisted of education and medical services and relief and development programs. Through such activities, they became a virtual state within a state. In some places, they became the only organizations that offered services which met people's needs.

They linked up with their international counterparts in both their advocacy and rendering of services (Ashworth 2004). The activities of both groups were complimentary. The local determination and dedication was matched by the external ones. Many advocacy groups had carried the issues far and wide. One can even claim that without this linkage of the local with the external, the effort would not have borne fruit. In the last analysis, the advocacy of FBOs inside and outside the country had generated far-reaching political influence that eventually led some countries to apply the necessary pressure to bring the warring factions to the negotiating table.

> When peace was finally brokered between South and North in the Sudan in January 2005, much of the credit went to Evangelicals like Franklin Graham, Billy Graham's son, who runs the mission organization's Samaritan's purse. He and his staff were all acquainted with the devastation in Sudan and one of the hospitals has been bombed repeatedly in the South. He put pressure on President George W. Bush to make ending the conflagration a diplomatic priority. (Bergner 2006: 2)

On the ground, churches were actively involved in the search for peace. Wherever violent conflicts flared in any part of the country, especially in the south, churches used their resources to find peaceful solutions. Besides the north-south war that was raging within the country, there were also other violent conflicts that pitted various communities against one another. The churches took it upon themselves to launch what they called "the People-to-People Peace-Making in Southern Sudan" (NSCC 2004).

One cannot go into the details of all the efforts that have been expended on this score. One only mentions a few. Initially, the churches addressed their relationship with the SPLA/M in 1997. The aim was to diffuse the growing antagonism between the churches and the movement. The two groups met in Yei, south Sudan, and arrived at agreements on many issues of common interest. By all accounts, this meeting was understood as laying the foundation for a peace agreement in Sudan. It also prepared the ground for tackling local intercommunal violence. The Dinka-Nuer West Bank Peace and Reconciliation Conference held from February 27 to March 8, 1999 in Wunlit, Bahr-el Ghazal, Sudan, was a very important example of how churches were really involved in the resolution of conflicts (NSCC 2004).

Such a trend in the search for peace was also prevalent in the capital, Khartoum. This is something fresh and interesting in the light of the fact that religion was and is still a force in the conduct of war in the country. Even so, there were attempts to use the same religion to work for peace. In this regard, one needs to point out the ground laid by the Comprehensive Peace Agreement (CPA) in January 2005. The agreement contains generous provisions or clauses regarding the society in general and religions in particular. It recognizes that Sudan is a multireligious, multicultural, and multiracial society. It therefore calls for respect of differences and tolerance among all concerned. It goes even further by exempting the south from being ruled by the *Sharia*, which is operative in the north. The CPA recognizes that "there shall be freedom of belief, worship and conscience for followers of all religions or beliefs or customs and no one shall be discriminated against on such grounds" (SIRC 2005: 4).

Taking its cue from these lofty aims, the Sudan Inter-Religious Council (SIRC) publicly declared its commitment to work for the implementation of these ideals. It further resolved to contribute its share in promoting the peaceful coexistence of the various religious groups in the country.[4] A witness to such an endeavor may be seen in the "dialogue meeting on the role of religious leaders in peace building" organized by the SIRC in cooperation with the US Institute of Peace in Khartoum July 25–26, 2005. There was broad agreement that religious leaders should

1. be peace makers;
2. approach the politicians with this mandate;
3. heal the wounds of society bruised by war;

4. become instruments in resolving   conflicts among warring parties;
5. support peace policies like the CPA;
6. organize dialogues among leading personalities;
7. spread the concept of religious tolerance; and
8. work jointly to address the plight of the poor, promote justice, reconciliation and forgiveness (SIRC 2005).

It is a very tall order indeed! Even so, one has to admit that there are people who have already taken the first steps. To begin with, they have come together from different religious and social backgrounds under very difficult circumstances. They have articulated some noble aims. They have attempted to disseminate them to the wider public. They have also committed themselves to work together to translate all of this into practice even in the face of seemingly huge challenges. And all this is done a few months after the end of a bloody and long war!

DEBATE IN THE PUBLIC SQUARE?

There are also fruitful discussions going on ostensibly through the contributions of Sudanese scholars. In one of the boldest pieces of argument on this very situation in Sudan, Mohammed Salih has plunged into the very discussion with exemplary boldness (2003: 96–120). He argues that the promulgation of *Sharia* as the law of the land has had serious repercussions. First, once it became part and parcel of the constitution, it would have serious consequences. It practically shuts the door to many people in the country who do not profess the Muslim faith. It went further and introduced unnecessary divisions on the people. "The introduction of sharia has become a source of schism between Arab and non-Arab Muslims as well as between Arab Muslims and African Christians" (Salih 2003: 104). It also divided the advocates of a secular political regime that accommodates all the varieties of ethnic and religious communities in the country. Many were worried that they would be effectively excluded from a "theocratic state." They would be rendered "second class citizens" in their own country because of their religious or political convictions. If one is to adhere to the Qur'anic dispensation as espoused by the party in power, the National Islamic Front (NIF), one would be constrained to affirm that non-Muslims would be relegated to an inferior status within the country. They would be subject to Muslim benevolence and not enjoy their intrinsic rights as equal citizens of a country.

Second, Salih also argues that there are divisions in the interpretation of Islam among various groups who adhere to the faith. In some cases, the interpretations do contradict one another; they do not agree on everything. Therefore, room must be given to a plurality of interpretations that have to live with one another. If they cannot, the consequences are dire.

> Internally, the diversity of Muslim orientations in terms of sects, brotherhood and *tariqa* makes it difficult for Sudanese to reconcile their different interpretations of the Qur'an. The case of Sudan becomes even more complex when different interpretations, forms and ideologies based on Islam are contested across political boundaries defined by one Muslim denomination or another. (Salih 2003: 118)

Third, regarding the application of *Sharia*, the question of harsh measures such as amputation of limbs, stoning of adulterers, and so on, which are incompatible with modern laws become problematic. Every single verdict and resultant punishment has the possibility of becoming "irrational" and thus antimodern. The conclusion of Salih is instructive in this regard: "As long as this situation continues, the rationality/irrationality embedded in the Qur'an (just as the rationality/irrationality embedded in any other religious text) is irreconcilable with the diversity of Muslim socio-economic and historical experiences or the secular rationality of the modern world" (Salih 2003: 119).

Fourth, the idea of the *umma,* which is important in Islam, becomes problematic. In Islamic thought, nations are artificial boundaries. The Muslim faithful are one entity; they are members of one religio-political community irrespective of where they live. There are no national boundaries that separate them. Therefore, a section of Islamic thought rejects the division of the Muslim faithful into different nationalities. The *umma* transcends such human creations. Under ideal circumstances, Muslims should live under the caliphate that brings the religious and political spheres under one God. In such a unitary regime, there is room for a rule only by God—theocracy.

The consequences of such a provision are dangerous, according to Salih: "This, in my view, makes authoritarian elitism (practiced by NIF leadership under the name of Islam) answerable only to God ... Privileging religious orthodoxy in interpreting the Muslim response to modernity in all its manifestations defies the reality of the contemporary Muslim world" (Ibid., 119). The ruling group in any given country will then have the ample opportunity to usurp power in the name of God. Since such a group has claimed to own the interpretative tools of the law in the name of the Divine, it alone has the authority and the exclusive right to know the difference between right and wrong. "If the state power is divine, then politics is not more than exercising God's will by an authoritarian Muslim elite that controls the state under the name of Islam" (Ibid.).

An-Na'im on his part makes his point in the context of human rights (2003: 25–48). In the cotemporary world, no one can exist outside a world that is ruled and guided by the concern for human rights. Therefore, peoples and states are bound by these human rights covenants that hover over every aspect of social and political relationships in the world. If one is to belong to and claim one's rightful place in this modern world, one cannot but give unswerving allegiance to these human rights agreements that should regulate human life.[5] Any contemporary life worth its name has to subject itself to and be judged by these universal guidelines. Any deviation from such a system renders any political dispensation suspect.

In line with Salih, An-Na'im argues that different interpretations of the religious imperative in the Muslim world have to be taken into consideration. One has to be mindful of the fact that Muslims have also been at odds with one another over the interpretation of their sacred texts. For example, they have differed on what the role of the state is and how it should be organized. As a result, they have often resorted to violent conflicts to practice their interpretation. This disagreement has a long history behind it. "The Islamic legitimacy of the state has always been a cause of conflict and civil war since the death of the Prophet Muhammad in 632." The enduring division between the Sunni and the Shia Muslims is a consequence of such a disagreement. In such a context, it is indeed impossible to impose *Sharia* law not only on non-Muslims but even on Muslims as well. "It is neither legally permissible nor practically viable for a group of Muslims to force even fellow Muslims, let alone non-Muslims, to accept and implement a specific view of *Sharia*, whether as a matter of state policy or informal communal practice." Since a difference of interpretation obtains within the Muslim world, there is no one interpretation that has to be applied overboard and under all circumstances. "In other words, significant disagreement about the content and application of *Sharia* is inherent in the system itself as understood and practiced by believers from the beginning." The end result is that disagreements should be the order of the day. Any party that imposes its specific understanding on others who do not share its opinion thus violates their rights.

The recommendation of such eminent scholars is that there should be room for agreement and disagreement. The prevalence of conflicting interpretations precludes any unilateral imposition of one's exclusive interpretation on others. In other words, the only way is to engage in a discussion in the public square and seek the truth together.

NIGERIA

Crossing to Nigeria, one finds that FBOs did find a niche to respond to the situation of violent conflicts. One of the most prominent efforts was initiated and run by a pastor and an imam. Their stories have now become world famous and they have toured the world to share their experiences. Before they came to work together, Pastor James Movel Wuye and Imam Muhammad Nurayn Ashafa were sworn enemies who set out to destroy each other as well as their respective followers. To this end, they had been involved in various activities that fuelled the violent conflicts that they led. In the process, Pastor Wuye even lost his arm in one of the violent confrontations. At a certain stage, however, they recognized the dead end to which their activities were leading them. Once they understood the futility of their determination to continue the conflicts, they found a new way. Their faith was at the center of this change of heart and the decision and determination to confront peace instead of war.

In a strange twist of events, the two began to meet. As the meetings continued for some years, they examined their faiths together and arrived at the conviction that violent conflicts lead nowhere. They concluded that they are truer to their respective faiths when they renounce violence and become agents of peace instead. Their intense collaboration extended in reaching out to other people and making a difference in situations caught up in conflicts that had a religious beginning.

Through their extensive writing and involvement, they have now established themselves as active and respected agents of conflict resolution. They have established a center in the very place where they used to fight in defense of their faiths. The Interfaith Mediation Centre/ Muslim-Christian Dialogue Forum based in Kaduna, Nigeria, has now become an established place for the publication of pamphlets, books on interfaith mediation and peace building (Van Tongeren et al. 2005: 226–232). They have also traveled far and wide to share their experiences with a wide range of people dealing with the issues of peace and conflicts and the contribution of the two faiths.

SIERRA LEONE

As the war raged in Sierra Leone, there were no winners. In the midst of this mayhem, there were several attempts to bring the fighting groups together and arrive at a peaceful resolution of the conflict. Nevertheless, the various rebel groups and the government could not agree on any common platform. Consequently, the war drugged on and on. It was at this stage that the involvement and contribution of the faith-based communities became crucial (Tesfai 2006: 55–66; Appleby 2000: 150–155; Lezhnev 2005: 25–49). The Inter-Religious Council of Sierra Leone (IRCSL) played a significant role in establishing contact with the warring parties and made possible the start of negotiations. The involvement of this council made up of Muslims and Christians contributed significantly to the rapprochement that was desperately needed among factions that had no clue as to how to engage in peace discussions. In this way, the council met a felt need that led somewhere. In this instance, we have another excellent example of a contribution to peace by religious groups who brought their resources together. Their understanding that their faiths were sources of peace and reconciliation enabled them to face the warring factions and to play the role of honest brokers and mediators.

When there was a dead end, when there was no military victory in sight, the president of the country felt it necessary to call for the engagement of the council. He appealed to them to be involved in a peace process. The council began to act as intermediary in initiating dialogue between the rebels and the government. It also persuaded the rebels to release some of their captives, especially women and children.

As the meetings gathered momentum, many other actors were also drawn into the peace process. Nongovernmental organizations (NGOs), the United Nations, the African Union, and the Economic Community of West African States (ECOWAS) were all pitching in. The involvement of such actors strengthened the hand of the council, which felt it could carry out its mandate. The rebels were brought to understand that there was a need for a peace process. They were persuaded to meet the government for talks. The two belligerents agreed to meet in Lome, Togo. The negotiations had started in earnest. A peace agreement was signed by the two parties in 1999. The various antagonists agreed to share the government portfolios. It took long before peace would become a reality.

In any event, the government was restored as a consequence of the peace deal. A government of national unity followed later. Some leaders of the rebel groups were included in the government and occupied key posts. For example, the leader of RUF, Foday Sankoh, was given an important post that amounted to the position of a vice president. He was also granted diplomatic immunity to protect him from being prosecuted for the crimes he committed during the civil war.

It was a bitter pill to swallow for many citizens. It seemed that after committing so many atrocities, the rebels were rewarded and protected. The council therefore took it upon itself to explain the agreement to the public. Its members crisscrossed the country to meet the people and to sensitize them regarding the meaning of the peace agreement that had been signed. The council had to play the important role of selling the peace agreement by acquainting the population with its contents. It used the media and organized training workshops on the issues of human rights. Among the trainees were *Imams* and Pastors who were usually close to the populace. They would then in turn disseminate what they had learned to their constituencies.

The council had to address the deep trauma that had been inflicted on the population. Entire villages had been destroyed as a result of the war. Many families had been divided. There was wholesale destruction. In some cases, people were herded into a hut and burned alive. There were also human skulls buried in mass graves. These graves witnessed that not only the dead but people were also buried alive. The people who witnessed and survived all these atrocities were so traumatized that they found it difficult to start a new life. The council thus took it upon itself to respond to the needs of the people. It tried to find ways and means of healing the people and assisting them to reconcile with their dreadful past.

In many villages, people saw the land as cursed as a result of the massacres that were committed there. In line with their religious worldview, the people found it difficult to till what they saw as cursed land and expect it to yield its fruits. They could not bring themselves to use a land where they saw the corpses of many people. In their view, the land was haunted and it had become the abode of evil. In accordance with the beliefs of the people, the land had to be cleansed and purified before they accept it as fit for agricultural activity. The council devised cleansing rituals that were applied on the areas concerned. Some of the places with grave memories were then turned into community centers. They became memorials to the grim history that lay behind them.

The council was also involved in the activities of the Truth and Reconciliation Commission. They toured the country to listen to the grievances of the people. They heard all the complaints and compiled them into a final report.

On the whole, the IRCSL played a very important role in the transition of the country from war to peace. First and foremost, it laid the ground for the encounter between the government and the rebels. The council became the instrument that earned the confidence of both. This is not an easy achievement in itself especially considering a brutal civil war that created mayhem on a vast scale. Second, the council became instrumental in leading the warring groups to the table of negotiations. And third, it worked hard to consolidate peace, healing, and reconciliation in a traumatized society.

UGANDA

Similar stories also emerge from other regions of the subcontinent. In the case of Uganda, one also witnesses some attempts by religious leaders to address the plight of their people (Khadiagala 2001: 1–12). Taking into consideration the situation of the country, the religious leaders in the areas that were hard hit by the war waged by the Lord's Resistance Army (LRA) rose to the occasion. They came together and decided to face the situation and try their hand in bringing peace. In the light of the violent history of Uganda, such a step in the search for peace was not easy.

The positive aspect of the religious leaders in this case was that they overcame their differences and forged a united front. The leaders in the north of the country transcended the various former divisions that hitherto characterized their relationships with one another. In this particular case, they took the conflict situation in their region into consideration and resolved to address it together. This was unprecedented in the history of the region. It was the first time that the leaders of the various denominations came together to do something about a situation in unison. As a result, the Acholi religious leaders assumed the responsibility of dealing with the conflict in their region. It was acknowledged by many that this was a groundbreaking move by religious leaders who were often attached to the sectarian views that also contributed to divisions in their communities.

These religious leaders eventually formed the Acholi Religious Leaders Peace Initiative (ARLPI) in 1997. It brought together the various leaders of the two main Christian groups, Catholics and Anglicans, as well as Muslims. Their main aim was to approach the leaders of the LRA with a peace proposal. Before doing so, however, they brought their respective followers closer to one another by using their considerable reach through their places of worship. They began by sharing their message of peace and reconciliation with their respective religious communities.

Once they consolidated their unity and strengthened their base, they approached the president of Uganda with a memorandum. Their main point was that reconciliation was essential in the attempt to bring a peaceful resolution to the problems that haunted Acholiland. In the end, the message was received by the president. The religious leaders were on their way to make their next move. They began to organize meetings among many concerned groups, including members of the government, the military, and other NGOs to garner broad support and to forge a united approach. Their main conclusion was that a military solution against the LRA would not work. As a result of their representations, the government accepted a ceasefire. Contacts were also established with the LRA.

One of the interesting steps the leaders took in order to strengthen their mediating position was to link up with the Acholi Diaspora and to use its resources and influence to make a difference in the work for peace. The fact was that some in the Ugandan Diaspora were supporting the LRA. The move by the religious leaders tempered this support and channeled it instead toward peace. At the instigation of the religious leaders, the government on its part went further by issuing an Amnesty Act. It was an unexpected success for their efforts.

As a basic strategy, the leaders tried to reach as many people as possible from all walks of life. They trained and created groups of volunteers who would work for peace. They extended their sensitization process by including instructions on such broad topics as human rights, reconciliation, and community development. Peace volunteers were instrumental in organizing people at the local level. Due to their efforts, people from all walks of life and different backgrounds were meeting locally and regularly to deal with all kinds of conflicts that arose within the communities. The leaders also shared their experiences with other neighboring communities that had experiences of being involved in violent conflicts. They also reached out for international assistance and support by making extensive contacts with international bodies and foreign governments. As a result of their efforts, dialogue touched many aspects of life. It influenced even the behavior of government officers. The overall result was that the involvement in the search for peace affected communities at different levels.

The next step was to approach the rebels with the intention of brining them into a peace process. This was privately initiated by some members of the religious leadership. Some of these initiatives began to bear some fruit. While expanding their network, they also presented demands that included, among others, the release of abducted children by the LRA. Some rebels even went so far as to ask for forgiveness and gave themselves up to the religious leaders. Taking all these various activities into consideration, the assessment of the work of the ARLPI is positive indeed: "The ARLPI is an innovative experiment in cross-confessional mobilization defying the history of sectarianism in the north and Uganda in general. An experiment in interfaith collaboration, it has thus far effectively used its ecumenical pedestal to agitate for peaceful approaches to the civil conflict" (Khadiagala 2001: 12).

Even though peace had not come as a result of the activities of the religious leaders, they had made an important contribution in engaging all levels of society in the direction of peace and coexistence.

IFAPA

There are also other interfaith initiatives that did not focus on specific areas but tried to address the conflict situations in the entire continent. This is the case with Inter-faith Action for Peace in Africa (IFAPA 2005). Initially organized by the Geneva-based Lutheran World Federation (LWF), it has taken the initiative of organizing a meeting of religious leaders to work for peace. Beginning from its first meeting in South Africa in October 2002, it has brought together representatives of a variety of confessional backgrounds, including African Traditional Religions, Bahai', Buddhism, Christianity, Islam, and Judaism. It has organized three international interfaith meetings that exchanged ideas, planned programmes, and came up with statements. Some of the important activities undertaken by the initiative are visits by leaders drawn from different religious communities and countries. They visit areas that are wracked by violent conflicts, meet the leaders and fighters in these places, listen to the suffering people, gain a better grasp of the situation, and explore the way of peace. They visited the DRC, Sudan, Sierra Leone, Liberia, among others. In their second meeting in South Africa, they launched what has been dubbed "A mother's campaign for a healthy Africa."

In its continuing quest to transcend religious and political boundaries and to entrench peace in the continent, IFAPA once again organized a meeting of religious leaders in Rwanda, the third in a series (Rieth 2006: 78–80). Once again, they represented a cross-section of leaders from a variety of religious confessions. This time round, they were a small number. They met in a symbolic venue—the Hotel of the Thousand Hills in Kigali, a place that had gained notoriety during the Rwanda genocide in 1994 when approximately 800,000 people perished in gruesome circumstances. In their own way, the religious leaders were searching to find ways and means of making peace possible in Africa in the context of gruesome events. As in other conferences, they prayed together in their own languages and traditions. They were neither aiming at overcoming their religious differences nor to convince one another of the truth or falsity of their religious stance. Their only aim was to see if they could find together the way to sustain and uphold peace in Africa. Some of the leaders came from areas that are fighting against one another. Even though they themselves came from areas that pitted their communities or countries against one another, they chose to find ways to dialogue and engage in a common adventure—the search for peace.

IFAPA has also thrown itself into translating the interreligious meetings into actions in support of development and service to others. To just refer to one example, it has taken the initiative of delivering water to some rural areas in Rwanda. "The IFAPA project will provide safe water to over 21,000 people in Gatore (Rwanda)." At the inauguration of the said project, the president of IFAPA and the LWF General Secretary, Dr. Ishmael Noko, declared: "The water project is a tangible result of IFAPA's work to encourage practical cooperation among African religious leaders and communities across the continent to promote peace and prevent conflict in Africa...Poverty and underdevelopment in Africa provide fertile ground for conflict, but religious leaders working together can play a crucial role in promoting development and peace in this continent." A local Muslim leader, Sheik Saleh Habimana added: "This project not only brings water to the people, but it also offers the rest of Africa and the world a model of harmonious interfaith co-operation for development and peace" (Wanjiku 2008: 8; Riungu 2008: 28).

ACRL

Another worthwhile initiative in this direction is the one organized under the African Council of Religious Leaders (ACRL)—Religions for Peace. This is related to the World Conference of Religions for Peace (Appleby 2000: 150–155).[6] It was conceived in 2002 and established officially in 2003. The council manifests profound interests and concern in poverty and violence and their effect on sustainable development. The Millennium Development Goals (MDGs) are widely discussed and kept in perspective in this connection. On its part, the council also has ambitious programmes. It aims to address a wide range of issues having to do with peace, human rights, orphans, vulnerable children, and overall sustainable development. To do so, it has established local chapters in the form of interfaith councils in twenty-six countries. The council also deals with Gender-Based Violence (GBV), Female Genital Mutilation (FGM), HIV/Aids, among others. The local councils also build regional meetings to deal with conflicts in conflict areas such as the Great Lakes Region, West Africa, and the Horn of Africa.

An important component of the ACRL is the African Women of Peace Network. In their turn, the women are involved in a variety of activities that have to do with peace and women's rights. They are important actors in peace building and conflict transformation. They form an integral part of delegations that visit areas of conflict, such as the one sent to Somaliland and Puntland (former regions of Somalia). One of the practical steps taken by ACRL is the provision of 150 bicycles to religious leaders in northern Uganda to facilitate their mobility in meeting the needs of orphans and children as well as their families. In their visits, the religious leaders also take part in the distribution of HIV/Aids drugs to an estimated 50,000 people in Uganda.

The declared intention of the ACRL is to face the challenge posed by violent conflicts. Some of the prominent activities of the ACRL in this regard are joint meetings, addressing the problems of conflict-ridden areas and visiting them, and making their concerted voices known through representation and issuance of statements. Regarding Zimbabwe, for instance, a delegation of religious leaders traveled to South Africa and met the Southern African Development Community (SADC)—appointed mediator of the peace talks, the former South African President Thabo Mbeki. They conveyed their concern about the deteriorating political and humanitarian situation in the country.

A fresh pursuit which is in the process of being developed is that of "shared security." To start with, even though there are marked differences within and among faith communities, ACRL affirms that there are widely shared common values. The idea is not to focus on the doctrines that separate the various faith communities. Rather, they have to lift up the basic human values that are intrinsic to and based on their beliefs. Among these are peace, humanitarian assistance, human rights, dignity, and collective development. Consequently, all these values are now being encapsulated in the concept of "shared security." It emphasizes the idea that, as human beings, we are all tied together. No one can be secure unless all are secure. The security of each and every individual depends on the security of all.

Another interesting development is reaching out northward to the Muslim/Arab world in ACRL's quest to extend the interreligious dialogue and cooperation. In this endeavor, they were guests of the Islamic Society of Libya in December 2008. A delegation of approximately 200 participants was hosted by the Libyans. The idea is to bring about an active involvement of the Muslim/Arab world in the work of the interfaith activity in the continent. In this connection, sub-Saharan Africa seems to have made great strides in building bridges among the various FBOs and found ways and means of making them work together. There is an intensive and strong cooperation among the leadership. In this sense, it may be said that it has blazed a trail.

PROCMURA

No presentation of peace initiatives would be complete without mentioning PROCMURA. One can in no way bypass the efforts and activities of what could be called a pioneer organization on this score. The Programme for Christian-Muslim Relations in Africa (PROCMURA), based in Nairobi, Kenya, has been active in searching ways and means of bringing about the rapprochements between the two major faiths in the continent. It has engaged itself for the last forty odd years in strengthening the relationships that should ideally exist between the adherents of the faiths. Its broader aims had been to bring about greater understanding between the faiths, especially Christianity and Islam, and to strengthen cooperation and life together. Through its various conferences and publications, courses and seminars, it has played a very important role in carrying out its special mandate.

To its credit, it was not only confined to the intellectual level. But, it also addressed real issues of conflict having to do with religion and their communities. In the words of its general advisor, the Rev. Dr. John Mbillah, it had been engaged in its own version of "quiet diplomacy" for a greater part of its existence, especially beginning from the 1990s. Wherever conflicts arose among and between faith communities, the programme took steps deemed appropriate to address them. It brought together Christian and Muslim leaders and dispatched them in joint peace missions. Violent conflicts in Sudan, Nigeria, Liberia, Sierra Leone, and other parts of Africa were objects of peace initiatives undertaken by the programme.

Recently, however, wide consultations that it had conducted regarding the relevance of its work lead it to give greater and urgent attention to the issues of violent conflicts in the continent (Mbillah 2008). According to its findings, these conflicts were crying out to be heard, seen, and addressed without delay. The leadership was gripped by the conviction that unless it turned its attention to this urgent task, the overall situation of the continent could deteriorate. Consequently, it took it upon itself to bring together and alert the leadership of the two major faiths to the emergency. It assumed the task of engaging the leaders in the search for and establishment of peace. To this end, it organized high level and important meetings of religious leaders. To begin with, it brought together leaders from the Great Lakes Region and the Horn of Africa. The other significant thing is that it also brought prominent politicians to give their views on the situation. Its reach was not confined to a limited area. Rather, it aims to include the entire continent in its future plans.

Important ideas and convictions have been highlighted in the meetings. It came to recognize one of the surprising facts. Although Africans are considered to be religious through and through, it is also religious people who are perpetrating wars and violence. This is due to the fact that religion has been used in a negative way by believers. There is ignorance and misunderstanding of the core values of the faith among their adherents. The participants in these meetings recognize that they have a "common mission to uphold and sustain peace." The leaders thus accept that it is incumbent upon them and falls within their responsibility to work for peace, mobilize their flock for this very purpose, build bridges, overcome misunderstandings which could generate violence, and create the conducive environment where conflict is prevented, resolved, and peace sustained. To this end, they would engage with all people, including politicians and governments, in influencing policies that promote coexistence, justice, reconciliation, and peace. The views expressed by Dr. Mbillah reflect the general leading convictions that informed the meetings:

> It is Christians and Muslims who interpret their respective scriptures of the Bible and the Qur'an respectively to promote peace or misinterpret it and call for war. People of faith can promote peace and peaceful coexistence in the continent if they do not talk about peace but work hard towards the securing of peace and endeavour to live in peace with one another. To collectively do this requires people of religion to talk to each other as we do here and will do in the last few days and not just about each other. It is in talking with each other that we can cooperate and collaborate, exercise positive tolerance, and constructively engage one another to help Africa to see itself and its people as a unity in variety. That unity can then link-up with the common humanity of the human family worldwide. (2008: 62)

The activities of IFAPA, ACRL, and PROCMURA are just glimpses into the activities through which initiatives for peace are being conducted in the continent. It is also instructive to note these initiatives cast their nets far and wide. They do not limit their activities to themselves only. Rather, they also try to reach out political and civic leaders who play important roles in shaping the direction of societies. They involve politicians such as parliamentarians and former national leaders in their deliberations.

In some cases, one cannot help but observe that their activities are duplicated. In many cases, they also involve the same religious leaders. For instance, one notes that while IFAPA met in Libya in November 2008, ACRL met in the same country in December. Nevertheless, at least so far, they seem to have found a modus vivendi that does not stand in the way of one or the other organization. They share in their committees and also exchange information. There is no question that bringing about a unified front would conserve a lot of resources, both human and material. It would also have contributed to greater efficacy in carrying out their mission of addressing violent conflicts and the establishment of peace in the subcontinent.

CONCLUDING REMARKS

In the first six chapters, we discussed about cases where religion played a role in fuelling war and violent conflicts. The countries which became victims of these wars have been adversely affected; they had been devastated. Their peoples have been displaced; many were killed. National lives have been shattered. From Southern Africa to Sudan, Nigeria, Ivory Coast, Uganda—we saw how these wars had created havoc in all aspects of life. Even the future of the countries was compromised.

As we contemplate the religion-inspired wars, we see four parts in this scenario. In the first scenario, we find that there is a religious battle within. The protagonists belong in the same camp. As far as religious adherence is concerned, they confess the same faith. For instance, if we take the South African case, the Boers and the majority of black Africans belonged to the same faith. They used the same scriptures and preached from the same book. They expounded their divergent theologies from exactly the same sources. In other words, they seemed to worship the same God while they interpreted this God differently. It is interesting to note that this is the case within both the Muslim and Christian faiths. We also saw that in Nigeria, various Muslim brotherhoods basing themselves on the same faith did not see each other eye to eye. As a result, they pitted their followers against one another and caused mayhem and destruction. They resorted to violent measures to make their point. In Uganda, the antagonism between the Anglican and Catholic wing of the Christian faith had far-reaching consequences in the history of the country. The political organization and direction informed by such religious divisions had adverse repercussions on the country. Such a disagreement among believers of the same faith is manifested in many places.

It must be admitted that, even in such situations where religion was at the center of a violent conflict, there were also some other factors that exacerbated the situation and contributed to the war effort. Racial and ethnic differences added fuel to the religious separation. In some cases, religion becomes an instrument of excluding the other who may be different on the basis of race or ethnicity. Without diminishing the role that religion plays in such a situation, the exclusion of the other on non-religious bases increases the stakes. In such situations, religion loses its integrity and becomes the tool of something else.

The second scenario is provided by Somalia. The scene is intriguing because of two important reasons. In the first, when we dealt with it, we saw how the country had one religion. It was united in living under one faith. As adherents to the same faith, one would expect that people would not have a divisive religious element that pitted them against one another. In a sense, one often said that they were privileged to belong to one religion. The fact of the matter is that they descended into chaos. For about two decades now, they have been engaged in a fratricidal war. Despite many efforts at reconciliation, they have not been able to pull themselves out of the catastrophe. Furthermore, their case becomes intriguing because they belong to the same stock. Unlike some other countries such as South Africa, Nigeria, or Uganda, which had been rocked by conflicts, the Somalis did not come from different racial or ethnic sources. They were united on many fronts. Somehow, all these valuable uniting factors could not hold the society together. Maybe the one factor of clan attachment proved more powerful in the end.

One is of course at a loss to find a plausible reason that explains why the conflict lasted so long in contrast to other places. One often refers to "clan politics" as the culprit. One hears the argument that the Somalis give more weight to the clan than to the nation, an idea contested by Nuruddin Farah, "Somalia's most accomplished and distinguished modern novelist" (Macbeth 2009: 102–105). In this connection, a question that arises is about the role of religion. The religion to which they adhered did not play a role, at least so far, in bringing them together. Why has the only faith to which the majority of the people adhere not provided a resolution to the conflict? In the light of the discussion on Somalia earlier, as in other cases, one would venture to say that the different interpretations of the faith by different factions have contributed to the continuation of the war. The dogged persistence of the internecine conflict may ultimately rest on the adherence of the parties to the conflict to a particular understanding of the faith in exclusion of the other. One poses the question of whether the different interpretations have become so irreconcilable that they have led their proponents to fight to the end. Such a fervent adherence to a faith rejects any compromise, being sure of the rightness of its position.

The third scenario is played out in places where there are a variety of religions. Whatever the number of adherents, the followers of the faiths disagree on some issues that they consider fundamental. They lift up their differences and find them irreconcilable. They label the antagonists their enemies. The only avenue open to them becomes violence. They find no other alternative but to attack their enemies and subdue them. This violent route becomes an act of faith.

Many parts of the subcontinent that we considered had become embroiled in such a debilitating situation. Once again, Nigeria is a good example of this religious division that ended up in violence. It is interesting to note that, sometimes, the religious reasons that lead to violent confrontations are not clearly enunciated. They are not clearly thought out as to whether they constitute breaches of the allegedly aggrieved faith to warrant such a violent reaction. It follows that relatively small incidents serve as causes for violent confrontations. Sometimes baseless rumors can serve as the causes of uncalled for violence. Whatever the incidents, one sees that adherents of different religions take it upon themselves to attack the faithful of a different religion. Cities are set on fire; people, including women and children, become victims of untold misery; property is destroyed.

The Horn of Africa was also the scene of a kind of a seesaw between Christians and Muslims. There is no question of the fact that the adherents of the two faiths had a tradition of coexistence. It is also true that there were violent conflicts between Christians and Muslims. At one time or another, the various states and mini-states—depending on the various periods and on who had more power—were often locked in violent conflicts. On the whole, the contemporary wars that are being waged in some parts of the Horn may have changed their name. One wonders whether the basic problems that operated in the past cast their shadow on the present. Even though the reasons for the conflicts are couched in contemporary terms, such as self-determination, liberation, and so on, one would not be off the mark if one surmises that the religious issues of yesteryear are still important and valid, to say the least. If so, they need to be addressed adequately to come to terms with the prevalent violence.

In this connection, one can also cite the war in Liberia and to a certain extent in Sierra Leone. The explicit pronouncement of Charles Taylor had shown that religion was also at the center of the civil war. The various fighters believed that they had God on their side. In other words, they were convinced that God was fighting with them and for them. As a matter of fact, they were carrying out God's divine plan by waging war. Irrespective of the destruction and human deaths they caused, they firmly believed that the Divine was in tune with them. We also saw that this religious inclination was in line with the religious worldview of Liberians in general. They believed that God held Liberia in his hands.

It followed that, in whatever they did and any activity they played a part in, God was involved. Ultimately, for good or for worse, it was not human beings who were masters of their destiny. Rather, it was God who ran human affairs. In the last analysis, no one was thus responsible for their actions. With such beliefs in the background, there is an unresolved spiritual issue that still lingers in Liberia even after the conclusion of the war. The ultimate resolution of the spiritual question would undoubtedly contribute to the reconciliation of the people with themselves. It would also highly contribute to a future of peace.

The fourth scenario was the places were conflicts were brewing. We saw how the countries in east Africa were sitting on a powder keg, so to speak. The voices of the various faith communities, in this case Christian and Muslim, are becoming increasingly shrill. In the three countries, reactions from one side or the other have brought attention to the growing tension. Some have warned of dire consequences. Some had even mentioned the specter of a violent conflict in the future. The sum total of it all is that the future has become uncertain with regard to the outcome.

A fifth scene that offers an interesting case study is Zambia. We have not raised the issue earlier. One cannot pass without referring to it because it offers an interesting case in sub-Saharan Africa. The avoidance of war and conflict in a situation that promotes a polity apparently infused by Christianity is significant. When the second president of the country, Frederick Chiluba, took power, one of the first measures he took was to proclaim Zambia a Christian nation. He even drew up a constitution in which such a proclamation became an integral part (Gifford 1998: 197).

It is of interest to note that there are intriguing elements in this story. The Christian churches in the country opposed the move. The question uppermost in their minds and which is perfectly reasonable is whether the proclamation of a "Christian state" will give a just and fair place to Zambians who are adherents of other religions. On the face of it, one would have expected the Christian churches to endorse wholeheartedly and without any reservation the move taken by the president. They would have seen it as a move to give them power and privilege as some churches did. On the contrary, the mainline churches opposed the decision and argued against it. The established churches in Zambia were simply up in arms against the promulgation. They did not share in the euphoria that accompanied it in some parts of the society. In other words, even with the proclamation, the opposite voice was not quashed. The churches simply did not accept that the religious establishment should swallow the political institutions. The churches argued consistently that church and state should remain separate. Their main argument was that it would send a wrong message to the non-Christian population of the country. They took into consideration the effect of the proclamation on other citizens of the nation. They expressed their conviction that the state has the duty not to exclude any of its citizens on the basis of religion. True to their fears, there were anti-Muslim speeches that were delivered by some leaders. Such developments cast a shadow on the future of peaceful coexistence of religions.

One has also to refer to another side of the story. Compared to predominantly Muslim societies, in this regard Egypt, such a proclamation in a country with a Christian majority hardly succeeds in deviating substantially from the "secular" bases of its political practices (Palmer 2003: 121–138). It forges on with the institutions of democracy, however flawed some of them may be. At least such a façade is maintained and is not erased by the adherence of the nation to a particular faith.

Writing in 2003, the Sudanese scholar An-Na'im wrote that "despite the history of *jihad* movements and present crisis, there is little indication of fundamentalist resurgence in postcolonial Sub-Saharan Africa except in the Sudan and Northern Nigeria" (2003: 31). In view of the evidence that we have presented so far, one concurs with this view at least at this juncture. One also has cause to wonder how long the statement will hold true. Whether in ongoing wars or simmering ones, one finds ample evidence to show that religion is becoming a source of violent conflicts. In East Africa and the Horn of Africa, religious militancy is gaining ground. There are voices that are insistently calling for a militant approach. There are even clashes in Mozambique and Malawi (in 1993, which incidentally had a Muslim leader). According to some observers, the case of Zanzibar is also posing a growing challenge to both Tanzania and the region as a whole in the long run.

As An-Na'im has plausibly argued, the rise of fundamentalism may have a lot to do with the political, social, and economic crises. When people become distraught and disappointed with the powers that be in the world, their only choice becomes the reversion to the divine. Only their religious worldview provides room for a religious interpretation of the state of affairs. They mostly see their plight as a case of divine disfavor. They become convinced that only repentance and reversion to the "true path" will restore the wellbeing of the people. When their world has collapsed right, left, and center and they see no hope on the horizon, the only hope for a better life becomes the otherworldly.

An extreme example may be offered from an incident in Uganda to explain the length to which desperate people can go to:

> In Kampala tongues are still wagging about a programme on the private FM station Simba on the night of February 18. It featured a woman called Nambi, who claimed to be God, who created the heavens and the earth. She claimed that since she created everything, she could heal everything. The host was very skeptical, but he let her have her say. Apparently Ugandans, burdened as many Africans are with poverty and many other miseries, didn't share the presenter's doubts. They called in large numbers asking for the address of her practice, and whether she can bring riches, help women find nice husbands, get children and cure impotence. (Onyango-Obbo 2007: 10)

With rampant poverty, high unemployment, hunger and malnutrition, diseases aplenty, and lack of overall human security, religion certainly becomes the only succor left for the people. Charlatans therefore have a field day. All kinds of religious "healers" stock the land. They offer their wares to bring about instant fame, wealth, political power, and other good things of life. As Ellis and Ter Haar pointed out, there is a great deal of confusion that gives rise to a myriad of uncertainties:

> After a century of rapid and profound change, there is considerable confusion about what precisely constitutes good and evil including in such important matters as making war, while in many countries there is no consensus on which authorities are competent to pronounce on such matters. The old techniques no longer work. Nowadays, the traditional spirit world itself is often seen as inherently evil. (2004: 95)

Be that as it may, one cannot lose sight of the material circumstances that have their bearing on religion. From the cases of violent conflicts that have been presented earlier, one sees how religion may contribute to either violent conflicts or peace. In all these situations, there is one fact that operates across the board. When it comes to war and peace, at the center of it all stands the issue of the interpretation of a given faith. Irrespective of whether one is inside or outside the faith, there are conflicting interpretations of the fundamentals of the faith that obtain. The fact is that they are the building blocks that are used in the construction of opposing identities, which lead to the rejection or acceptance of one another. The conflicting interpretations of the same faith lead to the conclusion that there is room or there is no room for the affirmation of a different interpretation. This is unfortunately replicated in many other places.

One sees that there are different interpretations of the faith that operate to give rise to violent conflicts. There are also interpretations that lend themselves to bring peace and entrench it. People go their separate ways depending on how they interpret the tenets of the faith. We saw how former sworn enemies in Nigeria became ambassadors of peace and reconciliation. Their deep enmity translated into deep friendship based on a different interpretation of the same scriptures. We also saw how the same logic operated in Sierra Leone. Christians and Muslims in the country together devoted themselves in the search for peace and the healing of the country ravaged by war. The initiatives IFAPA, ACRL, and PROCMURA, among others, on their part applied themselves to address the issues of war and peace. They brought religious leaders from across the religious divides and invited them to bring peace and healing to societies torn by war. Once again in this endeavor, the leaders were turning to their scriptures to find tools for peace. The ambivalence on the holy warrior/infidel was faced squarely. Even though the ultimate answer to the ambiguity is hidden in the bosom of the Divine and will haunt the people of faith till kingdom come, such leaders have the temerity to bring their faiths to the open and subject it to the scrutiny of others. In this manner, they offer the only possibility of transcending the dangerous dichotomy that threatens to tear societies apart. It does so by daring to bring the opposites together in the public square.

The one indispensable element in all these worthy attempts is the readiness and willingness by various actors from the same faith and from across the religious divide to engage in dialogue. Leaders within the confines and outside are led to believe that only genuine interaction with the holders of an opposite interpretation—whether with those inside or outside the boundary of the faith—is the way that eventually leads to coexistence, reconciliation, and cooperative work. It is the courage to put the differences in the public square, debate them openly and seek agreement or disagreement in good faith that ultimately guarantees a peaceful life together.

This is the profound lesson one gets especially from South Africa. The religious arguments in support of the policy of Apartheid were questioned from within and from without. There was a deep and intensive discussion of the faith and its policy implications in the public square. Internal and external players pitched in and engaged in vigorous debate. Finally, the majority reached a conclusion that led to the dismantlement of the policy.

One finds that in the various religions, there are antecedents of mechanisms of public discourse. In the Christian tradition, there are cases of ecumenical councils. They dealt with a particular doctrinal issue that turned out to be burning and divisive within the Christian community at a given point in time. The leadership came from far and wide, met in one place and deliberated on the issue at hand. In the end, they came up with some sort of a consensus, which they put in writing. These decisions would serve as guidelines on the issue that became controversial in the first place. There is also a Muslim tradition that is relevant in this connection. The *Shura* (consultation) is, in principle, a very important instrument of engaging various points of view as it concerns an issue of faith. It is a forum for deliberations that discusses issues of critical concern to the community of faith. The result is made known and the guidance given after a process of debate on the matter at hand. In this connection, there is also the possibility that may open up with *tajdid* and *ijtihad*. As Yusuf Fadl Hasan proposes: "[There is the] the necessity to open widely the door of *ijtihad* (independent deduction by method of analogy from the Qura'n and the Sunna), so that all the competent *'ulama* (scholars in Islamic sciences) could discuss, rationalize and harmonize their findings through consultations" (2002: 40).

No one can deny that, in both cases, the mechanisms are often hijacked by some leaders. They do not seem to go down to the grassroots level and involve the ordinary folk. They may more often than not be confined to the elite. They are also politicized. Parties in the conflict fight it out to defend and protect their interests. In the process, the main idea of the forum may be compromised. Even so, one cannot dismiss them outright in view of their misuse. They can be revived and used with the best intentions for the best results.There is no question that with the resurgence of religion, there is also what Peter David has called an "authority deficit" even on the religious plane (David 2007: 14). This fact will weigh heavily and negatively on any religious leader who will look beyond the different interpretations and bring all concerned together. Fortunately enough, as we have seen earlier, there are intrepid souls who are applying themselves to this very task. One cannot but refer to the example offered by the Nobel Laureate Archbishop Desmond Tutu on the sub-Saharan region and beyond. His story is an eloquent example of many other religious leaders in the subcontinent who may not have reached his global stature but have made a difference in their own way in their own sphere of influence. In this connection, the role played by religious leaders in many sub-Saharan African countries in the process of transition from dictatorship to democracy and in reconciling societies in the process is nothing less than amazing. In many cases, they literally stood between national collapse and finding a new way for a given society to maintain its sanity and unity in diversity (Tozy in Ellis 1996: 59; Hizkias and Wachira 1996). It is also encouraging to note that such local endeavors are being supplemented and strengthened by calls on the global level.

On the international level, the Organization of Islamic Conference (OIC) in its recent meeting held in Senegal has called for holding a serious dialogue among Christians and Muslims. There are also a number of other initiatives on different levels, including one on the level of the United Nations (*Economist* 2007: 67; 2008: 63). To succeed in this endeavor, there are three basic tenets to which the protagonists and participants should adhere, in line with the arguments of R. Scott Appleby.

> If religions are to play a significant peace building role in the twenty-first century, their leaders must pursue three interrelated goals: First, religious communities must be engaged, consistently and substantively, in the international discourse of rights and responsibilities... Second, religious traditions with strong missionary outreach must promote missiologies, or theologies of mission, that foster respect for universal human rights norms, including the right to religious freedom. All religious traditions, in turn, must encourage the practice of civic tolerance of religious outsiders, including the revivalists and proselytizers among them... Finally, religious leaders must give priority to establishing and supporting ecumenical and inter-religious dialogues and cooperative ventures designed to prevent or transform conflicts that are based on religious or cultural disputes. (2000: 245; 2003: 197–229)

For better or for worse, one can no longer deny the fact that religion has become a force that should be reckoned with in the contemporary world. No longer can it be ignored. We have also seen that this strength of religion tilts toward violence in many cases. The confrontation of religious identities often gives rise to violent conflicts. In this reclaimed and new found position of power, the holy warrior/infidel holds center stage. The dangerous ambivalence can only be mitigated, if not eliminated, through the courage wielded by religious leaders to bring forth such an attempt at clarity to the public square.

We have seen how religious leaders in Africa have taken such a step on various levels. They have become important voices in different countries. Such was the case in Nigeria, Sierra Leone, and Sudan. One finds that significant discussion is going on among scholars on the very issue of religion and politics even in Sudan. The role of religion in public life is on the public agenda. This is a healthy development.

In connection with the global effort, there are four advantages from sub-Saharan Africa that could and should be used positively by religious leaders. First, religion is still a powerful force in society. Without neglecting and downplaying its disruptive and negative side, one observes that people are very religious indeed. Religion continues to offer meaning to people's lives. They adhere to it in droves. Used well by its leaders, this situation can be utilized effectively for positive ends. Second, as we have observed, it could be said that, on the whole, full scale wars have not erupted in the region because of religion. The exceptions to date are Nigeria, Somalia, and Sudan. This is a valuable asset that should be preserved as much as possible. All concerned, leaders and followers of given religions alike, have to do everything possible in their power to maintain it and use its potential effectively. Third, religious leaders in the subcontinent have something going for them in this regard. As we saw earlier, they are held in high esteem by the followers of their respective religions. They are more respected than their political counterparts. Their words and leadership positions carry a great deal of authority. In times of crises, they obviously tend to lose their grip on the situation. There are complaints that, sometimes, religious leaders may not be up to the task of playing the role of peacemakers expected of them. They may instead fall into the trap of fuelling conflicts. Still, there is no gainsaying their authority. If they rise to the task, and if they are fully aware of the responsibility they carry in the society, as they have done on many occasions, they possess resources that can be used to offer responsible leadership in periods that are characterized by multiple crises. They can thus play the role of the much needed peacemaker and guide in a world that is increasingly threatened by the holy warrior/infidel.

Fourth, in many cases, religious leaders have come forth to profess their faith in difficult circumstances. This demands a lot of courage and determination. For them, it is an act of faith. Some of them have even given up their lives for such a cause. Some of them had also been exiled and ostracized for their activities. Many had held on to make a difference. Their unequivocal stance in support of peace finally helped to transcend the ambivalence of the holy warrior/infidel to bring about peace.

NOTES

PREFACE

1. "About the Global Partnership for the Prevention of Armed Conflict," see van Tongeren 2005: 695. www.gppac.net

1 RELIGION AND RACIAL DIFFERENCES IN THE SOUTH

1. *"Apartheid* was a new term but an old idea. It literally means 'apartness', and it represented the codification in one oppressive system of all the laws and regulations that had kept the Africans in an inferior position to whites for centuries...The premise of Apartheid was that whites were superior to Africans...The policy was supported by the Dutch Reformed Church which furnished Apartheid with its religious underpinnings by suggesting that Afrikaners were God's chosen people and that blacks were a subservient people. In the Afrikaner's worldview, apartheid and church went hand in hand." Mandela 1994: 127–128.

2 RELIGION AND POLITICAL DIFFERENCES IN THE NORTH

1. "Profile: Omer El Bashir, president of Sudan" *Africa Report*, No. 9, January 2008, p. 147.
2. Human Rights Watch/Africa, *Behind the Red Line*, p. 273. Quoted in Hasan and Gray 2002: 89, 90.
3. "Sudan MPs pass law on unity treaty" *Daily Nation*, July 7, 2005, p. 14.

3 RELIGION AND VIOLENT CONFLICTS IN THE WEST

1. "Six killed in attacks on Muslims" *Daily Nation*, February 22, 2006, p. 14.
2. Ibid.
3. "Cote d'Ivoir" *Africa Review 2005*, p. 91.
4. "Simone Gbagbo—the steel behind the throne" *The Africa Report, Africa in 2008*, No. 9, January–March 2008, p. 168.

4 RELIGION AND SIMMERING VIOLENCE IN THE EAST

1. *Daily Nation*, December 20, 2006, p. 19.

5 POLARIZATION OF RELIGIOUS-POLITICAL GROUPS IN THE HORN OF AFRICA

1. See the valuable contributions on the Horn in De Waal 2004. Unfortunately, I got hold of the book only after the completion of the manuscript and its submission to the publisher.

6 VIOLENCE AND ISLAM'S CHALLENGE IN SOMALIA

1. For example, he ignores the Sunni/Shia divide ("what can only be called a 'Muslim Civil War'") and its role in the crisis in the Middle East and elsewhere and deals with the conflicts from a unitary Christian (West)/ Muslim confrontation only. See, for example, Mai Yamani, "Sunni-Shia divide widens into civil strife" *Daily Nation*, July 21, 2006, p. 9.
2. But see the interesting discussion in Ahmed 1995.
3. "Power vacuum in Somalia as factions fight" *The East African,* March 26–April 1, 2007, p. 18.
4. Abdi Ismail Samatar, "The Islamic Courts and the Mogadishu Miracle: What Comes Next for Somalia?" *Review of African Political Economy* (Fall 2006, I quote from an advance copy. The pages of the quotations from this source are included in the body of the text).
5. "Somalia: step carefully now!" Editorial, *The East African,* September 25–October 1, 2006, p. 12. Smith 2007: 44.
6. The view of the special envoy of the UN Secretary General to Somalia, for example, is clear: "Mr. Ahmedou Ould Abdallah wants Somalia's elite, including politicians, to keep off the delicate process of electing the war-torn country's new leader...He said the elite were responsible for the political and leadership mess in the Horn of Africa country for the last two decades." Godffrey Olali, "UN official warns elite to keep off electing Somali president" *Daily Nation,* January 7, 2009, p. 20.
7. Adel Darwish in *al-Sharq al-Awsat* quoted in Abdi 2007: 34.
8. "Teacher elected new Somali president" *Sunday Standard*, February 1, 2009, p. 31.

7 INITIATION INTO PEACE

1. "Police catch witchdoctor at poll tribunal" *Daily Nation*, September 28, 2007, p. 23.
2. See the Web sites of the Netherlands Institute of International Relations "Clingendael" and of the Life and Peace Institute and Uppsala University

on the same subject and the publications *Tools for Peace: Life and Peace in a Globally Changing World*. Proceedings of the International Ecumenical Consultation, October 8–12, 2003, Uppsala, Sweden. *Tools for Peace? The Role of Religion in Conflicts*. Report from an international Interreligious peace conference, November 21–24, 2004, Soederkoeping, Sweden.

3. "Faiths move to stem communal violence" *Sunday Nation*, September 16, 2007, p. 31.

4. Sudan Inter-Religious Council (SIRC), Memorandum of Association, n.d.

5. "The question of the consistency of Islam with modern norms brings to mind a remark made during the General Assembly debate of the Universal Declaration by Pakistan's first foreign minister. Zafralla Khan said he was voting in favour because he felt the Qur'an compelled him to do so. During the same debate, however, the Saudi Arabian representative delivered a fiery speech condemning the Universal Declaration outright as an anti-Islamic document. What an extraordinary exhibition of the two facets of Islam." Khalil 2002: 70. Banning 2005: 215.

6. www.wcrp.org

BIBLIOGRAPHY

Abbay, Alemseged, "Diversity and Democracy in Ethiopia" *Journal of Eastern African Studies*, vol. 3, no. 2, July 2009, pp. 175–201

Abdi, Rashid, "Unveiling the Islamists" *BBC Focus on Africa*, October–December 2006, vol. 17

———, "Africa's Afghanistan" *BBC Focus on Africa*, January–March 2007, vol. 18, no. 1

Abdullah, Ibrahim, and Patrick Muana, "The Revolutionary United Front of Sierra Leone" In Clapham, *African Guerillas*, pp. 172–193

Abir, Mordechai, *Ethiopia: The Era of the Princes: The Challenge of Islam and the Re-unification of the Christian Empire 1769–1855* (London: Longmans, 1968)

Adebajo, Adekeye, "West Africa's Tragic Twins: Building Peace in Liberia and Sierra Leone" In *Building Sustainable Peace*, edited by Tom Keating and W. Andy Knight (Tokyo: United Nations University Press, 2004)

Agutu, Mark, "Kenyans score on patriotism: poll says people proud of country" *Daily Nation*, September 16, 2005

Ahmed, Abdusamad, "Popular Islam in Twentieth-Century Africa: The Muslims of Gondar, 1900–1935" In Samatar, *In the Shadow of Conquest*, pp. 102–116

Ahmed, Ali Jimale, ed., *The Invention of Somalia* (Lawrenceville, NJ: Red Sea Press, 1995)

Alden, Chris, *Mozambique and the Reconstruction of the New African State: From Negotiations to Nation Building* (New York: Palgrave Macmillan, 2001)

Ali Abdel Gadir Ali, and Ibrahim A. Elbadawi, "Prospects for Sustainable Peace and Post-Conflict Economic Growth in the Sudan" In *Post-Conflict Economy in Africa*, edited by Augustin Kwasi Fosu and Paul Collier (New York: Palgrave Macmillan, 2005), pp. 143–161

Ali Abdel Gadir Ali, Ibrahim A. Elbadawi, and Atta El-Batahani, "Sudan's Civil War: Why Has It Prevailed for So Long?" In Collier and Sambanis, *Understanding Civil War*, pp. 193–219

Allen, John, *Rabble-Rouser for Peace: The Authorized Biography of Desmond Tutu* (London: Random House, 2006)

An-Na'im, Abdullahi Ahmed, "Islamic Fundamentalism and Social Change: Neither the 'end of history' Nor a 'clash of civilizations'" In Ter Harr and Busuttil, *The Freedom to do God's Will*, pp. 25–48

Appleby, R. Scott, *The Ambivalence of the Sacred: Religion, Violence and Reconciliation* (London: Rowman & Littlefield, 2000)

———, "Religions, Human Rights and Social Change" In Ter Haar and Busuttil, *The Freedom to Do God's Will*, pp. 197–229

Ashafa, Muhammad Nurayn, and Movel Wuye, *The Pastor and the Imam* (Ibadan, Nigeria: Ibrash Publications Centre, 1999)

Ashworth, John, *Five Years of Sudan Focal Point: Briefings* (Pretoria: Sudan Focal Point—Africa, 2004)

———, *Inside Sudan: The Story of People-to-People Peacemaking in Southern Sudan* (Nairobi, Kenya: The New Sudan Council of Churches [NSCC], 2003)

Ayman, Abu, "Yes, anti-Muslim bias is rampant" *Daily Nation*, December 14, 2007

Badal, Raphael K., *Local Traditional Structures in Sudan* (Nairobi: Life and Peace Institute, 2006)

Bafadhil, Abdurahman, "Let's keep religion out of politics" *Daily Nation*, August 30, 2007

Bahru, Zewde, "What did we dream? What did we achieve? And where are we heading?" *Africa Insight*, vol. 34, no. 1, June 2002

Banjo, Adewale Segun, "Nigeria: An Overview of Multi-faceted Conflict" In *Through Fire with Water: The Roots for Division and the Potential for Reconciliation in Africa*, edited by Eric Doxtader and Charles Villa-Vicencio (Cape Town, South Africa: Institute for Justice and Reconciliation, 2003), pp. 89–106

Barnes, Cedric, "The Somali Youth League, Ethiopian Somalis and the Greater Somalia Idea, c. 1946–48" *Journal of Eastern African Studies*, vol. 1, no. 2, 277–291, July 2007

Barnes, Cedric, and Harun Hassan, "The Rise and Fall of Mogadishu's Islamic Courts" *Journal of Eastern African Studies*, vol. 1, no. 2, 151–160, July 2007

Barret, David, George T. Kurian, and Todd M. Johnson, eds., *World Christian Encyclopedia: A Comparative Survey of Churches and Religions in the Modern World*, second edition (Oxford: Oxford University Press, 2001)

Behrend, Heike, "The Holy Spirit Movement and the Forces of Nature in the North of Uganda 1985–1987" In Hansen and Twaddle, *Religion and Politics in East Africa*, pp. 59–71

———, "War in Northern Uganda: The Holy Spirit Movement of Alice Lakwena, Severino Lukoyo and Joseph Kony (1986–1997)" In, Clapham *African Guerillas*, 107–118

Bemath, Abdul S., "The Sayyid and Saalihiya Tariga Reformist, Anticolonial Hero in Somalia" In Samatar, *In the Shadow of Conquest*, pp. 33–47

Benson, G. P., "Ideological Politics versus Biblical Hermeneutics: Kenya's Protestant Churches and the Nyayo State" In Hansen and Twaddle, *Religion and Politics in East Africa*, pp. 177–199

Bergner, Daniel, "A family's mission of faith in Kenya" *International Herald Tribune,* Monday, January 30, 2006

Berkeley, Bill, *The Graves Are Not Yet Full: Race, Tribe and Power in the Heart of Africa* (New York: Basic Books, 2001)

Bill, Barnabas, and Peter Ngetich, "Raid on displaced families that shocked the world" *Sunday Nation*, January 6, 2008

Billheimer, Robert S., *Breakthrough: The Emergence of the Ecumenical Tradition* (Grand Rapids, MI: Wm. B. Eerdmans, 1989)

Blakely, Thomas D, Walter E. A. van Beek, and Dennis L. Thompson, eds., *Religion in Africa* (London: James Currey, 1994)

Briggs, John, Amba Oduyoye, and Tsetsis, George, eds., *A History of the Ecumenical Movement,* vol. 3, 1968–2000 (Geneva: World Council of Churches, 2004)

Buwembo, Joachim, "Peace returns to Uganda after half century of military trauma" *The East African*, March 10–16, 2008

Calderisi, Robert, *The Trouble with Africa: Why Foreign Aid Isn't Working* (New York: Palgrave Macmillan, 2007)

Ceresko, Anthony R., *Introduction to the Old Testament: A Liberation Perspective* (Maryknoll, NY: Orbis Books, 1992)

Chabal, Patrick, and Jean-Pascal Daloz, *Africa Works: Disorder as Political Instrument* (London: James Currey, 1999)

Chande, Abdi, "Radicalism and Reform in East Africa" In Levtzion and Pouwels, *The History of Islam in Africa*, pp. 349–369

Chipenda, José, "Namibia: A Sign of Hope?" In *Religion and Politics in Southern Africa,* edited by Carl Fredrick Hallencreutz and Mai Palmberg (Uppsala: The Scandinavian Institute of African Studies, 1991)

Clapham, Christopher, ed., *African Guerillas* (Oxford: James Currey, 1998)

Collier, Paul, and Nicholas Sambanis, eds., *Understanding Civil War, Evidence and Analysis, Volume 1: Africa* (Washington, DC: The World Bank, 2005)

Dallas, Gregor, *Poisoned Peace 1945: The War That Never Ended* (London: John Murray, 2005)

David, Peter, "The Authority Deficit" *The Economist*, The World in 2007, 21st edition, pp. 14–15

Davidson, Basil, *Africa in History: Themes and Outlines* (London: Phoenix, 1992, Revised and expanded edition)

De Gruchy, John, W., "The Church and the Struggle for a Democratic South Africa" In Prozesky, *Christianity amidst Apartheid: Selected Perspectives on the Church in South Africa*, pp. 219–232

———, *Christianity and Democracy* (Cambridge: Cambridge University Press, 1995)

De Waal, M. A. Alex, ed., *Islamism and Its Enemies in the Horn of Africa* (London: Hurst, 2004)

Deng, Francis, M. *War of Visions: Conflict of Identities in the Sudan* (Washington DC: Brookings Institution, 1995)

Dobson, John, H., *A Guide to Exodus* (London: SPCK, sixth impression, 2002)

Doxtader, Eric, and Charles Villa-Vicencio, eds., *Through Fire with Water: The Roots for Division and the Potential for Reconciliation in Africa* (Cape Town, SA: Institute for Justice and Reconciliation, 2003)

The Economist, "Powerful Women in Africa" December 18, 2004

———, "Somalia, by the dawn the Islamists were gone" January 6, 2007

———, "In God's name: A special report on religion and public life" November 3, 2007

El-Batahani, Atta, "Sudan's Involvement in the Horn" In *Networking with a View to Promoting Peace: Towards Sustainable Peace—Civil Society Dialogue Forum for the Horn of Africa*. Nairobi, December 10–13, 2000. Second Conference Documentation (Heinrich Boell Foundation, Horn of Africa, 2001)

Ellis, Stephen, "Liberia's warlord insurgency" In Clapham, *African Guerillas*, pp. 155–171

———, *The Masks of Anarchy: The Destruction of Liberia and the Religious Dimension of an African Civil War* (London: Hurst, 1999)

——— ed., *Africa Now: People, Policies and Institutions* (London: James Currey, 1996)

Ellis, Stephen and Gerrie Ter Haar, *Worlds of Power: Religious Thought and Political Practice in Africa* (London: Hurst, 2004)

Eluemunor, Tony, "Why the disaster that Cote d'Ivoir became should serve as an eye-opener to Kenya" *Daily Nation*, State of the Nation, February 22, 2008

Fosu, Augustin Kwasi, and Paul Collier, eds., *Post-Conflict Economy in Africa* (New York: Palgrave Macmillan, 2005)

French, Howard W., *A Continent for the Taking: The Tragedy and Hope of Africa* (New York: Vintage Books, 2005)

Friedman, Thomas L., *From Beirut to Jerusalem* (New York: Anchor Books, 1995)

Garang, John, *"This Convention is Sovereign"* Opening and Closing Speeches, n.d.

Geschiere, Peter, *The Modernity of Witchcraft: Politics and the Occult in Postcolonial Africa,* translated from the French by P. Geschiere and Janet Reitman (London: University Press of Virginia, 1997)

Gifford, Paul, *African Christianity: Its Public Role* (London: Hurst, 1998)

Gofwen, R. I., *Religious Conflicts in Northern Nigeria: The Throes of Two Decades 1980–2000* (Kaduna: Human Rights Monitor, 2004)

Goldsmith, Paul, "Sharia law marks a sea change as Sharif woos Somali militias" *The East African,* March 9–15, 2009

Hansen, Holger Bernt, and M. Twaddle, eds., *Uganda Now: Between Decay* and *Development* (Oxford: James Currey, 1995)

———, *Religion and Politics in East Africa: The Period since Independence* (Oxford: James Currey, 1995)

Hasan, Yusuf Fadl, and Richard Gray, eds., *Religion and Conflict in Sudan* (Nairobi, Kenya: Paulines Publications Africa, 2002)

Hasbani, Nadim, "Soudan: L'insupportable complicite des Arabes avec Khartoum" Al Hayat, reprinted in *Courrier Internationale,* No. 856, 29.03–04.04.2007

Hassen, Mohammed, "Islam as a resistance ideology among the Oromo of Ethiopia" In Samatar, *In the Shadow of Conquest,* pp. 75–101

Haynes, Jeff, *Religion and Politics in Africa* (London: Zed Books, 1996)

Heinrich, Wolfgang, *Building the Peace: Experiences and Reflections of Collaborative Peace-Building, the Case of Somalia,* second edition (Uppsala: Life and Peace Institute, 2006)

Hinson, David F., *Old Testament Introduction 1, History of Israel,* revised edition (London: SPCK, 1990)

Hiskett, Mervyn, *The Course of Islam in Africa* (Edinburgh: Edinburgh University Press, 1994)

Hizkias, Assefa, and George Wachira, eds., *Peacemaking and Democratisation in Africa: Theoretical Perspectives and Church Initiatives* (Nairobi: East African Educational Publishers, 1996)

Holcomb, Bonnie K., and Sisai Ibssa, *The Invention of Ethiopia* (Trenton, NJ: Red Sea Press, 1990)

Holt, P. M., and M. W. Daly, *A History of the Sudan: From the Coming of Islam to the Present Day,* fourth edition (London: Longman, 1988)

The Holy Bible, Revised Standard Version (London: Oxford University Press, 1946)

Hope, Marjorie, and James Young, eds., *The South African Churches in a Revolutionary Situation* (Maryknoll, NY: Orbis Books, 1983)

Huntington, Samuel P., *The Clash of Civilizations and the Making of World Order* (London: Simon and Schuster, 2002)

———, *Who Are We? America's Great Debate* (London: Free Press, 2005)

Inter-Faith Action for Peace in Africa: *Collected IFAPA Documents and Reports* (Geneva, LWF, 2005)

International Crisis Group, *God, Oil and Country: Changing the Logic of War in the Sudan,* ICG Africa Report No. 39 (Brussels: ICG Press, 2002)

———, *Somalia's Islamists,* Africa Report No. 100–12 December 2005a

———, *Understanding Islamism,* Middle East/North Africa Report No. 37, March 2, 2005b

International Crisis Group, *Somalia: To Move beyond the Failed State*, Africa Report No. 147, December 23, 2008

Johnson, Douglass, H., *The Root Causes of Sudan's Civil Wars* (Oxford: James Currey, 2003)

Johnson-Sirleaf, Ellen, "There is some hope for Africa" *Daily Nation*, June 12, 2007

Juergensmeyer, Mark, *Terror in the Mind of God: The Global Rise of Religious Violence*, third edition updated (Berkeley: University of California Press, 2003)

Kaba, Lansine, "Islam in West Africa: Radicalization and the New Ethic of Disagreement, 1960–1990" In Levtzion and Pouwels, *The History of Islam in Africa*, pp. 189–208

Kalinaki, Daniel, "Kony comes in from the cold" *The East African*, September 4–10, 2006

Kapteijns, Lidwien, "Ethiopia and the Horn of Africa" In Levtzion and Pouwels, *The History of Islam in Africa*, pp. 227–250

Kasozi, A. B. K., *The Social Origins of Violence in Uganda 1964–1985* (Kampala, Uganda: Fountain, 1994)

———, "Christian-Muslim Inputs into Public Policy Formation in Kenya, Tanzania and Uganda" In Hansen and Twaddle, *Religion and Politics in East Africa*, pp. 223–246

Kastfelt, Niels, ed., *Scriptural Politics: The Bible and Koran as Political Models in the Middle East and Africa* (London: Hurst, 2003)

———, *Religion and African Civil Wars* (London: Hurst, 2005)

Keating, Tom, and W. Andy Knight, eds., *Building Sustainable Peace* (Tokyo: United Nations University Press, 2004)

Kepel, Gilles, *The Revenge of God: The Resurgence of Islam, Christianity and Judaism in the Modern World*. Translated from the French by Alan Braley (Cambridge, MA: Polity Press, 1994).

———, *La Revenche de Dieu* (Paris: Editions du Seuil, 1991)

Khadiagala, Gilbert M., "Greater Horn of Africa (GHA) Peace Building Project: *The Role of the Acholi Religious Leaders Peace Initiative (ARLPI) in Peace-Building in Northern Uganda*" mimeo. Handouts Presented at USAID/MSI, GHA workshop, Nairobi, January 17–19, 2001

Khalif, Abdulkadir, "Internal conflict over regional role is cause of Somali conflict" *The East African*, April 18–24, 2005

———, "New Somali president guaranteed nightmares from hard-core Islamists," *Daily Nation*, February 27, 2009

Khalil, Mohamed Ibrahim, "Human rights and Islamization of the Sudan legal system" In Fadl and Gray, *Religion and Conflict in Sudan*, pp. 58–71

Kokole, Omari H., "Idi Amin, 'the Nubi', & Islam in Ugandan Politics 1971–1979" In Hansen and Twaddle, eds., *Religion and Politics in East Africa*, pp. 45–55

————, "Religion in Afro-Arab relations: Islam and Cultural Changes in Modern Africa" In *Islam in Africa*, Alkali, Adamu, Yadudu, Motem and Salihi, eds., pp. 232–246

Kwayera, Juma, "Upheaval in Zanzibar is a threat to region's stability" *Sunday Standard,* May 18, 2008, p. 36

Lamb, David, *The Africans* (New York: Vintage Books, 1987)

————, *The Arabs: Journeys beyond the Mirage*, second edition (New York: Vintage Books, 2002)

Lambeck, Michael, ed., *A Reader in the Anthropology of Religion* (Oxford: Blackwell, 2002)

Lassky, Nicholas, José Miguez Bonino, John S. Pobee, Tom F. Stransky, Geoffrey Wainwright, and Pauline Webb, eds., *Dictionary of the Ecumenical Movement* (Geneva: WCC Publications, 2002)

Levtzion, Nehemiah, and Randall L. Pouwels, eds., *The History of Islam in Africa* (Oxford: James Currey, 2000)

Lewis, Bernard, *The Crisis of Islam: Holy War and Unholy Terror* (London: A Phoenix Paperback, 2004)

Lewis, I. M. ed., *Nationalism and Self-determination in the Horn of Africa* (London: Ithaca Press, 1983)

————, *A Modern History of the Somali*, revised, updated and expanded, East African Studies (Oxford: James Currey, 2002)

Lezhnev, Sasha, *Crafting Peace: Strategies to Deal with Warlords in Collapsing States* (London: Lexington Books, 2005)

Lone, Salim, "Toppling model Islamist rule could spark violent conflict" *Daily Nation*, May 4, 2007, p. 11

Lusk, Gill, "Horn of Africa, Eye of the Storm" *BBC Focus on Africa*, July–September 2007, vol. 18, no. 3

Macbeth, Alex, "Interview Nuruddin Farah, Somali author and journalist" *The Africa Report*, No. 14, December 2008–January 2009

Maimela, Simon S., "The Suffering of Human Divisions and the Cross" In *The Scandal of a Crucified World: Perspectives on the Cross and Suffering* edited by Yacob Tesfai (Maryknoll, NY: Orbis Books, 1994), pp. 36–47

Mandela, Nelson, *Long Walk to Freedom: The Autobiography of Nelson Mandela* (London: Abacus, 1995)

Mandivenga, Ephraim, "The Role of Islam in Southern Africa" In Hallencreutz and Palmberg, *Religion and Politics in Southern Africa*, pp. 74–84

Marcus, Harold G., *A History of Ethiopia,* updated edition (Berkeley: University of California Press, 2002)

Mbillah, Johnson, A., ed., *A Journey of Peace*: Report of a Conference on Religion and Conflict Prevention, Peace Building and Reconciliation in Eastern Africa, Dar-es-Salaam, Tanzania 2008 (Nairobi: PROCMURA, 2008)

Mbiti, John, *African Religions and Philosophy* (Nairobi: East African Educational Publishers, 1994)

Mbuvi, Jackson, "Conflict in Somalia: How to avoid Africa's Taliban next door" *Daily Nation*, January 05, 2007

Meredith, Martin, *In The Name of Apartheid: South Africa in the Postwar Period* (New York: Harper and Row, 1988)

———, *The State of Africa: A History of Fifty Years of Independence* (London: Free Press, 2005)

———, *Diamonds, Gold and War: The Making of South Africa* (London: Pocket Books, 2007)

Miles, William F. S., "Religious Pluralism in Northern Nigeria" In Levtzion and Pouwels, *The History of Islam in Africa*, pp. 209–224

Moorcraft, Paul L., *African Nemesis: War and Revolution in Southern Africa (1945–2010)* (London: Grassey's [UK], 1994)

Mpinganjira, Ernest, "Religionism: A threat to East African unity" *Sunday Standard*, March 30, 2008

Mufuruki, Ali, "Blind with power and ambition, they cannot see the fires" *Daily Nation*, February 22, 2008

Mugambi, J. N. K., and Mary N. Gatui, eds., *Religion in East Africa under Globalization* (Nairobi: Action, 2004)

Mukhtar, Mohamed Haj, "Islam in Somali history: fact or fiction?" In Ahmed, *The Invention of Somalia*, pp. 1–15

Mutua, Makau, "Massacre: Hypocrisy unveiled as Darfur death toll rise" *Sunday Nation*, December 3, 2006

Mwazemba, John, "Does Mugabe's style reflect the continent's predisposition?" *Saturday Standard*, June 28, 2008

NSCC, *Building Hope for Peace inside Sudan: People-people Peacemaking Process, Methodologies and Concepts among Communities of Southern Sudan* (Nairobi: New Sudan Council of Churches [NSCC], 2004)

Networking with a view to promoting peace: towards sustainable peace—civil society dialogue forum for the Horn of Africa. Nairobi, 10–13 December, 2000. Second Conference Documentation (Heinrich Boell Foundation, Horn of Africa, 2001)

Nura, Alkali, Adamu Adamu, Awwal Yadudu, Rashid Motem, and Haruna Salihi, eds., *Islam in Africa: Proceedings of the Islam in Africa Conference* (Ibadan: Spectrum Books, 1993)

Farah, Nuruddin, "How 'Maqal-disho' lost its innocence" *Daily Nation*, July 22, 2005

Nyama, Peter Adwok, *Politics of Liberation in South Sudan: an Insider's View*, second edition (Kampala, Uganda: Fountain, 2000)

O'Brien, Donald B. Cruise, "Coping with the Christians: The Muslim Predicament in Kenya" In Hansen and Twaddle, *Religion and Politics in East Africa*, pp. 200–219

Odde, Arye, *Islam and Politics in Kenya* (London: Lynne Rienner, 2000)

Odunfa, Sola, "Kano Chaos" *BBC Focus on Africa* July–September 2004, vol. 15, no. 3

———, "General Decline" *BBC Focus on Africa,* July–September 2006, vol. 17, no. 3

O'Fahey, R. S., "The Past in the Present: The Issue of the Sharia in the Sudan" In Hansen and Twaddle, *Religion and Politics in East Africa,* pp. 32–44

Oluoch, Fred, "A man of the people" *The East African,* September 11–17, 2006, pp. i, iv, v

———, "After the fall of Kismayu, will Baidoa be Islamists' next target?" *The East African,* October 2–8, 2006

Omanga, Beauttah, "Muslims urge action on Somalia" *Sunday Standard,* April 27, 2008

Onyango-Obbo, Charles, "Will Somalia be the final battle between Islam and the West?" *The East African,* October 16–22, 2006

———, "LRA knows what Besigye didn't; you must pose a military threat" *The East African,* November 4–11, 2007

Oshidari, Kenro, and Felix Bamezon, "Darfur crisis snowballing across central Africa" *The East African,* April 2–8, 2007

Ouazani, Cherif, "Les verites—d'Ismail Omar Guelleh" *Jeune Afrique,* No. 2395, December 3–9, 2006

Oyugi, Walter O., E. S. Odhiambo Atieno, Michael Chege, and Afrifa K. Gitonga, eds., *Democratic Theory and Practice in Africa* (London: James Currey, 1988)

Palmer, Monte, "The Qur'an and the Bible as Models of Politics: The Contrasting Experience of Zambia and Egypt" In Kastfelt, *Scriptural Politics,* pp. 121–138

Pankhurst, Richard, *The Ethiopians: A History* (Oxford: Blackwell, 2001)

Paye-Layleh, Jonathan, "Cleansed" *BBC Focus on Africa,* October–December 2006, vol. 17, no. 4

Kimani, Peter, "Somalia: Theatre of proxy wars and hidden agendas," *Daily Nation,* January 04, 2007

Polgreen, Lydia (*New York Times*), "Ivorian youth leaders want UN, French military out" *The East African,* January 23–29, 2006

Pool, David, "The Eritrean People's Liberation Front" In Clapham, *African Guerillas,* pp. 19–35

Presler, Judith, and Sally J. Scholz, *Peace Making: Lessons from the Past Visions for the Future* (Amsterdam: Rodopi, 2000)

Prozensky, Martin, ed., *Christianity amidst Apartheid: Selected Perspectives on the Church in South Africa* (London: Macmillan, 1990)

Reuters, "Gaddafi claim over Darfur" *Daily Nation,* November 20, 2006, p. 14

Reuters, "Amnesty criticizes Arabs over Darfur" *Daily Nation,* September 15, 2006, p. 18

Richburg, Keith, B., *Out of America: A Black Man Confronts Africa* (New York: A Harvest Book, 1998)

Rieth, Klaus, "Ausbrueche zum Frieden gelingen nur gemeinsam: interreligioese Konferenz in Kigali" *Der Ueberblick*: Zeitschrift fuer oekumenische Begegnung und Internationale Zusammenarbeit, 3/2006, September

Riungu, Catherine, "Inter-faith group launches water project in Rwanda" *The East African*, May 5–11, 2008

Robinson, T. H., "The History of Israel" In "The Book of Exodus" In *The Interpreter's Bible*, Vol. I, edited by J. Coert Rylaarsdam (Nashville, TN: Abingdon Press, 1990)

Rubenson, Sven, *The Survival of Ethiopian Independence* (London: Heinemann, 1976)

Salih, M. A. Mohammed, *African Democracies and African Politics* (London: Pluto Press, 2001)

———, "The Bible, the Qur'an and the Coflict in South Sudan" In Kastfelt, *Scriptural Politics*, pp. 96–120

Samatar, Abdi Ismail, "Back to the future" *BBC Focus on Africa*, July–September 2008, vol. 19, no. 3

Samatar, Said, S., ed., *In the Shadow of Conquest: Islam in Colonial Northeast Africa* (Trenton, NJ: Red Sea Press, 1992)

———, "Sheik Uweys Muhammad of Baraawe, 1847–1909, Mystic and Reformer in East Africa" In Samatar, *In the Shadow of Conquest*, pp. 48–74

Sanders, Edmund, "Fight over land keeps migrants on the move" *Daily Nation*, August 17, 2007

Sani, Shehu, "By Divine Right" *BBC Focus on Africa*, October–December 2008, vol. 19, no. 4

Sanneh, Lamin, *West African Christianity: The Religious Impact* (Maryknoll, NY: Orbis Books, 1983)

Sidahmed, Abdel Salam, "The Unholy War: *Jihad* and the Conflict in the Sudan" In Fadl and Gray, *Religion and Conflict in Sudan*, pp. 83–96

Sjollema, Baldwin, art. "Programme to Combat Racism" In *Dictionary of the Ecumenical Movement*, Lassky, et al. editors, pp. 935–937

Smith, Patrick, "Interview, Ali Mazrui: A danger of mushrooming enthusiasms" *The Africa Report*, No. 6, April 2007

———, "Somalia: A people held hostage" *The Africa Report*, No. 12, August–September 2008

Sperling, David C., and Jose H. Kagabo, "The Coastal Hinterland and Interior of East Africa" In Levtzion and Pouwels, *The History of Islam in Africa*, pp. 273–302

Stenger, Fritz, Joseph Wandera, and Paul Hannon, eds., *Christian-Muslim Co-existence in Eastern Africa*, Tangaza occasional papers/No. 22 (Nairobi: Paulines Publications, 2008)

Sudan Ecumenical Forum Assembly 2003: *International Advocacy for Peace in the Sudan* (Pretoria: Sudan Focal Point, 2003)

Sudan Inter-Religious Council (SICC), *Religion in the Comprehensive Peace Agreement* (Khartoum: Graphic Printing Company, May 2005)

———, SICC in cooperation with United States Institute of Peace: Recommendations of the dialogue on: *The Role of Religious Leaders in Peace-Building in Sudan*, held in Khartoum, July 25–26, 2005

Stavenhagen, Rodolfo, *Ethnic Conflicts and the Nation-State* (London: Macmillan, 1996)

Szulc, Tad, *Fidel: A Critical Portrait* (London: Hodder and Stoughton, Coronet Books, 1989)

Ter Haar, Gerrie, "Religious Fundamentalism and Social Change" In *The Freedom to Do God's Will: Religious Fundamentalism and Social Change*, edited by Gerrie ter Haar and James J. Busuttil (London: Routledge, 2003), pp. 1–24

Tesfai, Yacob, ed., *The Scandal of a Crucified World: Perspectives on the Cross and Suffering* (Maryknoll, NY: Orbis Books, 1994)

———, *Liberation and Orthodoxy* (Maryknoll, NY: Orbis Books, 1996)

——— ed., *Justice, Peace and Reconciliation for Post-war New Sudan: Report of an Inter-faith Consultation* (Nairobi Life and Peace Institute/Horn of Africa Programme, 2006)

———, "Foreword to the 2006 edition" In Heinrich, *Building the Peace*, pp. ii–v

Thatiah, Peter, "Gitari: The conscience of society is wounded" *The Standard*, July 8, 2008

Throup, David, "Render unto Caesar the things that are Caesar's: The Politics of Church-State Conflict in Kenya, 1978–1990" In Hansen and Twaddle, *Religion and Politics in East Africa*, pp. 143–176

Trimingham, J. Spencer, *Islam in Ethiopia* (London: Frank Cass, 1965)

Twaddle, Michael, "The Character of Politico-Religious Conflict in Eastern Africa" In Hansen and Twaddle, *Religion and Politics in East Africa*, pp. 1–15

Van Tongeren, Paul, Malin Brink, Marte Hellema, and Juliette Verhoeven, eds., *People Building Peace II: Successful Stories of Civil Society* (London: Lynne Rienner, 2005)

Villa-Vicencio, Charles. Art. 'Apartheid' In Lassky, *Dictionary of the Ecumenical Movement* pp. 44–45

———, *Trapped in Apartheid: A Socio-Theological History of the English-Speaking Churches* (Maryknoll, NY: Orbis Books, 1988)

Villa-Vicencio, Charles, and John W. de Gruchy, eds., *Apartheid Is a Heresy* (Grand Rapids, MI: Wm. B. Eerdmans, 1983)

Wachu, Adan, "Islam linked to terrorism? No way, it's a religion of peace and love" *Sunday Nation*, August 3, 2008

Waihenya, Waithaka, *The Mediator: Gen. Lazaro Sumbeiywo and the Southern Sudan Peace Process* (Nairobi: Kenway Publications, 2006)

Waliggo, John Mary, "The Catholic Church and the Root-Cause of Political Instability in Uganda" In Hansen and Twaddle, *Religion and Politics in East Africa*, pp. 106–119

Wamari, Elly, "A life he would rather forget" *Daily Nation,* Weekend, May 2, 2008

Wanjiku, Rose, "Rwanda forges ahead" *Saturday Standard,* April 12, 2008

Ward, Kevin, "The Church of Uganda amidst Conflict" In Hansen and Twaddle, *Religion and Politics in East Africa*, pp. 72–105

Warigi, Gitau, "Why battle for Muslim vote is so highly charged" *Daily Nation,* October 21, 2007

Wijsen, Frans, and Bernardin Mfumbusa, *Seeds of Conflict: Religious Tensions in Tanzania* (Nairobi: Paulines Publications, 2004)

Wiseman, John A., ed., *Democracy and Political Change in Sub-Saharan Africa* (London: Routledge, 1995)

Woldegiorgis, Dawit, *Red Tears: War, Famine and Revolution in Ethiopia* (Trenton, NJ: Red Sea Press, 1989)

Wrong, Michela, *I Didn't Do It for You: How the World Betrayed a Small African Nation* (London: Fourth Estate, 2005)

Yoder, John Howard, *The Politics of Jesus: Visit Agnus Nester,* second edition (Grand Rapids, MI: Wm. B. Eerdmans, 1994)

Young, John, "The Tigray People's Liberation Front" In Clapham, *African Guerillas*, pp. 36–52

Yousif, Mahmoud E., "Social Peace in Islam and the Post-War Sudan" In Tesfai, *Justice, Peace and Reconciliation for Post-War New Sudan*, pp. 45–51

Zinn, Annalisa, "Theory versus Reality: Civil War Onset and Avoidance in Nigeria since 1960" In Collier and Sambanis, *Understanding Civil War*, pp. 89–121

INDEX